I0881609

Praise for *Each in Our Own Language*

Durheim's book will deepen your understanding of rural life and ministry. *Each in Our Own Language* highlights the work of significant authors who address small-town and rural settings, as well as the dynamics of ministry in those contexts. Utilizing a variety of disciplines, he also explores, with a goal of helping people flourish, the many layers of symbolic meaning around language regarding rural life and social ethics.

—Jon Anderson, director of rural ministry, Luther Seminary

Benjamin Durheim takes everyday life in rural agrarian and small-town America as the starting point for a thoughtful and provocative theological exploration of symbolization, social ethics, human communication, and relationality. Durheim reminds us of our ongoing need to develop, expand, and practice skills in social literacy—that is, the practice of reading and responding to the varied symbols that mediate our integral human connectedness. This skill and its practice are crucial, laying the groundwork for both ethical action and communal worship, and for sustaining our grasp of what it means to live together on the way to God's reign.

—M. Shawn Copeland, professor emerita, Boston College

In our unfortunate era, when runaway rhetoric seizing upon others' words largely produces more heat than light, Benjamin Durheim invites readers to think through the symbol-mediated realities of social bodies to comprehend better how and why a people shares values and convictions. Durheim integrates critical theories of symbol, ritual, and aesthetics with freshly considered theological categories to enlighten efforts at self- and mutual understanding, ethical reflection, and societal solidarity.

—Bruce T. Morrill, SJ, Edward A. Malloy Chair in Roman Catholic Studies and Distinguished Professor of Theology, Vanderbilt University; author of *Practical Sacramental Theology: At the Intersection of Liturgy and Ethics*

In a world too comfortable with stereotyping, polarization, and instrumental thinking, Benjamin Durheim's boundary-breaking work in contextual rural theology could not be more timely or more welcome. Rooted in ethnographic research and the honest, loving gaze of Durheim's own rural living, *Each in Our Own Language* is rich with insight into symbol, liturgy, and the opportunities for sin and grace found in communities of neighbors and fellow believers. A must-read for anyone seeking to understand the past, present, and future of Christianity in North America.

—Kate Ward, associate professor, Marquette University

EACH IN OUR OWN LANGUAGE

EACH IN OUR OWN LANGUAGE

Symbolization and Social Ethics in Rural America

BENJAMIN DURHEIM

FORTRESS PRESS
Minneapolis

EACH IN OUR OWN LANGUAGE
Symbolization and Social Ethics in Rural America

30 29 28 27 26 25 1 2 3 4 5 6 7 8 9

Library of Congress Cataloging-in-Publication Data

Names: Durheim, Benjamin, author.
Title: Each in our own language : symbolization and social ethics in rural America / Benjamin Durheim.
Description: Minneapolis : Fortress Press, [2025] | Includes bibliographical references and index. |
Identifiers: LCCN 2025006489 (print) | LCCN 2025006490 (ebook) | ISBN 9781506498157 (paperback) | ISBN 9781506498164 (ebook)
Subjects: LCSH: Rural churches—United States. | Country life—Religious aspects—Christianity. | Signs and symbols—Religious aspects—Christianity. | Signs and symbols—United States. | Christian sociology—United States | Social ethics—United States. | United States—Rural conditions. | United States—Religious life and customs.
Classification: LCC BV638 .D87 2025 (print) | LCC BV638 (ebook)
LC record available at https://lccn.loc.gov/2025006489
LC ebook record available at https://lccn.loc.gov/2025006490

Cover image: Cover design by Faceout Studio, Amanda Hudson
Cover design: Faceout Studio

Print ISBN: 978-1-5064-9815-7
eBook ISBN: 978-1-5064-9816-4

For Paul Gunderson, whose delight in rural life helped form my appreciation of its beauty

CONTENTS

II
Rural Symbolization and Social Ethics

PREFACE

> *Now there were devout Jews from every people under heaven living in Jerusalem. And at this sound the crowd gathered and was bewildered, because each one heard them speaking in the native language of each. Amazed and astonished, they asked, "Are not all these who are speaking Galileans? And how is it that we hear, each of us, in our own native language? Parthians, Medes, Elamites, and residents of Mesopotamia, Judea and Cappadocia, Pontus and Asia, Phrygia and Pamphylia, Egypt and the parts of Libya belonging to Cyrene, and visitors from Rome, both Jews and proselytes, Cretans and Arabs—in our own languages we hear them speaking about God's deeds of power." All were amazed and perplexed, saying to one another, "What does this mean?*
>
> —*Acts 2:5–12, NRSVUE*

Sometimes I am amazed at what a gift it is to be able to understand one another. To share in sound and gesture, entering a common world of meaning in which presence is mediated from one to others and returned again, can be a truly beautiful thing. Participating in meaning-making together is a deeply human experience, made possible by many layers of linguistic encounter. Misunderstanding, then, is an equally human experience, one in which an encounter misfires in its shared meanings—sometimes badly—leading to exchanged untruths that complicate and often enough even toxify social space. This leaves to the side those situations in which malice and ill intent make misunderstanding a goal. Even in cases of the best intentions and efforts, misunderstanding can infect discourse like a virus, at times precipitating an immediate social malaise and at other times lying dormant until some stimulus brings it to the surface, and it causes social pain. Misunderstanding is not rare, but it is rarely benign.

The practice of understanding, however, is itself a multilayered endeavor. Those gathered in the story from Acts were not necessarily astounded by *what* they were hearing; they were astonished that they were hearing it in their own native languages. Expressing something close to the fullness of meaning in a language other than one's mother tongue can be a daunting challenge. The difficulty goes beyond grammar, usage, and vocabulary; some concepts, connotations, idioms, and layers of meaning do not translate well and may even be ultimately untranslatable, accessible only by those who have some level of fluency in the original language. In the liminal space between expression and reception of meaning, this negotiation between understanding and misunderstanding unfolds. Those witnessing the Pentecost event did not just hear automata uttering sounds they knew and could interpret; they received the message as from those intimately familiar with how things are said in Mesopotamia, Cappadocia, Phrygia, and the other locations recorded in the book. The speakers, given speech by the Holy Spirit, sounded like they knew the *homes* of those present. They did not just use words; they invited encounter and shared meaning.

When this book began taking shape in 2022, I was involved in conversations at Saint John's School of Theology/ Seminary regarding how to approach rural ministry and the preparation of ministers and professionals undertaking it. At the core of those conversations and those that have followed (flowering into courses, immersion programs, grant initiatives, and a host of engagement with rural ministry) was the conviction that helping to form ministers for work in rural contexts was about more than simply providing occasions to consider the contours of rural and small-town life. It was about facilitating encounter with the social realities that overlap in rural and small-town contexts and approaching them with a full set of contextual methodological tools.

More than once in my classes and conversations, people—particularly those whose experiences have largely been nonrural—have expressed a certain level of exasperation with the way politics and social issues are discussed in rural contexts. Why particular words or concepts take on the connotations they do, and why others do not seem to evoke the meanings they do elsewhere, is a persistent challenge (this has included everything from hot-button issues like abortion and gun control to more general social-ethical concepts like social justice). It is both easy and inaccurate to reduce rural discourse on pertinent or divisive social-ethical issues to the machinations of partisan politics, backward or regressive thinking opposed to healthy change, or simple old-fashioned bigotry. Some of each of these can be present in rural social contexts just as in nonrural ones, but the differences between rural and nonrural approaches to social realities, religious practices, political issues, and social ethics belies a reduction to one-dimensional consideration of these challenges. There is a depth to rural social reality (and to all social reality) that runs beyond what we mean when we speak to *how* we make meaning when we interact.

This book is an attempt to plumb that depth, to examine how the process of symbolization develops and mediates social contexts such that social reality—particularly that of rural contexts—can become more social-ethically legible. It is a work done from a theological perspective but engages contributions from sociology, history, political science, and ritual studies. My goal in this is in no way to "fix" rural discourse or social-ethical perspectives; such endeavors are already frustratingly common, attempting to reduce rural America to a set of problems to be addressed. My goal is to work toward illuminating how rural social reality makes meaning so that misunderstanding becomes rarer and understanding more common, more familiar. An essential aspect of that task, in my view, is to give due consideration to how symbols function in the constitutions of social contexts, paving the way for speaking and hearing truths not just in minimally adequate universalized discourse but in contextually accurate ways that open social-ethical discourse to shared ground and clarity. My hope, ultimately, is that we may hear one another each, truly, in our own language.

ACKNOWLEDGMENTS

In pursuing this project, I am deeply indebted to the many friends, colleagues, family members, and conversation partners who have helped support me as I worked through the processes of moving the research, analysis, and writing to completion. With thanks to God for bringing such people into my life, I am so very grateful for and humbled by the ways I have been blessed in the commiserations, encouragements, and challenges I have received throughout the process of writing this book.

The inception of this project was a reorienting of my work during the COVID-19 pandemic to focus on rural approaches to theology and ministry. In helping me discern this refocus, I am thankful to all my colleagues at the College of Saint Benedict / Saint John's University, particularly those in the theology department and the School of Theology/Seminary, whose support and insight helped me move into this area of scholarship with vigor. As the idea for the project took shape, I applied for and was granted collaborative research funding to work with undergraduate students at CSB/SJU to pursue ethnographic and qualitative research of rural Christian congregations; I express my thanks to the hardworking and diligent folks at CSB/SJU's Office for Undergraduate Research and Scholars, as well as to the undergraduate students who collaborated with me so enthusiastically during summers 2022 and 2023, Lydia Mattern and Gilbert Perez. To those churches and Christian liturgical communities who welcomed us into your spaces to do our research, many thanks for your hospitality and generous candor.

To test the waters for this project, the Critical Theories and Liturgical Studies seminar at the North American Academy of Liturgy graciously welcomed me to introduce and outline the work, and I am profoundly grateful to the members of that seminar for the vigorous scholarly conversations that unfolded in that set of meetings. In particular, I am grateful for the wisdom and encouragement given to me by Kimberly Hope Belcher, David Turnbloom, Layla Karst, Kristine Suna-Koro, Gerald Liu, Katrina Olson, Audrey Seah, Tony Alonso, Stephanie Budwey, and Sarah Johnson. When the writing began, I was privileged to be included in a writing group whose collaboration was both edifying and stimulating; thank you, Nicole Reibe and David Turnbloom, for sharing your processes and work with me. Throughout the process of writing, I have been blessed with input from those whose work has immersed them in rural Christian ministry and theology, and to them I extend my heartfelt thanks, especially Jon Anderson and Bernie Evans.

I have been fortunate to have this work interface well with other initiatives at my institutional home of Saint John's School of Theology and Seminary. To the directors of the *Conversatio* and *Sustained Encuentro* grants, Donelle Poling and Daniella Zsupan-Jerome, thank you for welcoming my work on rural ministry into your own professional worlds, and all of us share in gratitude to the Lilly Foundation for its funding of these grants. To the staff and student collaborators who worked with me to craft the rural immersion program at the SOT/Sem, which partly inspired areas of this book, thank you so much for your hard work and tenacity: Fabiano Adderly, Kelly Brueske, Patricia Weishaar, and all those in diverse areas of the university who helped make the programming a success. Additionally, I am deeply grateful for all the hard work that the team at Fortress Press invested in bringing this project to completion, particularly Laura Gifford, who walked with me from proposal to publishing, Kris Easler Miller, whose collaboration with Faceout Studio gave us the book cover, and Chantelle Gibbs, who worked with me through the final stages of the project. I also express sincere thanks to my family—my parents, grandparents, and children—who dealt so patiently with me as I spent the many mornings, afternoons, weekends, and hours of all kinds pulling this work together and were so generous in sharing their own stories, perspectives, and experiences of rural life.

Finally, to my spouse, Tara, I wish to say a most fervent and humble thank-you. You saw every aspect of this project—the difficult parts, the rewarding parts, the stressful parts, and the edifying parts—and you gifted me unwavering care and wisdom throughout the long wandering from idea to book. This book would not have been possible without your gentle counsel, shrewd editorial eye, and unfailing support. I love you and thank you.

INTRODUCTION

In his book *Everyone Must Eat*, Mark L. Yackel-Juleen relates a story about ministering as a pastor during the 1993 floods in the upper Midwest of the United States and witnessing the effects they had on many farmers.[1] The rain and floods that year had washed out huge swaths of crop land and prevented many other crops from maturing, making a harvest all but impossible for many parts of an area that had already been struggling economically for more than a decade and a half. One major political and social response to this disaster was, as one might hope, economic aid, in this case grounded in a program called Zero-92, which was aimed at paying farmers for crops that had been flooded out based on the value of the crops in the previous year.[2] Essentially, farmers would destroy the economically worthless crops (plow the fields under) and thereby access the aid payment—a difficult action to take, as Yackel-Juleen describes:

> On that dark and overcast day, my neighbor stopped to visit Shalom Hill Farm (SHF) where I lived and worked in southwestern Minnesota, and the subject quickly turned to the harvest. He pointed to the field adjacent to our place and said, "For thirty years I have farmed that piece of land and have taken what the Lord has given me—good or bad, mostly good. Now I am supposed to tell the Lord it's not good enough and plow it

---

1. See Mark L. Yackel-Juleen, *Everyone Must Eat: Food, Sustainability, and Ministry* (Fortress, 2021), 41–43.

2. Yackel-Juleen, *Everyone Must Eat*, 41–43.

> under . . . Pastor Mark, I just can't do it." . . . One man, having made the decision to plow under his crop and take the aid payment, made one pass through his field with the plow, got out of his tractor, and vomited. The act of destroying something he had worked so hard to create and care for overwhelmed him and made him physically ill.[3]

When social change or social action takes place, whether in the political, religious, or other spheres, the full meaning of the change or action often depends on the overlapping symbolic systems that give depth to the contexts in which they occur. Put differently, symbolization underwrites social ethics. In language, gesture, gathering, image, architecture, and most especially bodies (though this list could go on), humans swim in social realities that are deeper than the discursive or conceptual definitions layered on them. To investigate and work with the structures of human social life and try to form them toward the good is to depend in that work on systems of symbols both implicit and explicit, symbols that sustain and symbols that drive change, symbols that write identity on the social bodies that ethics interrogates. This fundamental conviction drives this project at the confluence of Christian liturgical/sacramental theology and social ethics. When social structures (and prescriptions regarding them) move and develop, it is systems of symbols and processes of symbolization that mediate the changes. Additionally, it is symbolization that had spoken those structures into existence in the first place, constituting by mediation of symbols a shared social space that resists reduction to its observable surface. The flesh of society moves only where the bones of its symbolic order can allow.

In the story of the 1993 floods, a structural response intended to mitigate economic hardship—the Zero-92 program—did so by the mechanism of requiring its participants to take actions (actively destroying failed crops) that carried meaning far beyond a utilitarian satisfaction of prerequisites for receiving relief. The symbolic reality of plowing crops under without harvesting them, even if they were

3. Yackel-Juleen, *Everyone Must Eat*, 41–42.

economically worthless, mediated religious and social distress that may seem odd or outsized unless one is able to read the symbolic systems at work in Midwestern agrarian life. This dissonance is exacerbated by the fact that the preexisting Zero-92 program, from a political perspective at least, likely made perfect sense to politicians as a structure through which to address the 1993 floods. It was not a new program in 1993; it had been used through the 1980s to mitigate costs associated with farm surpluses,[4] so no new structures needed to be crafted. Zero-92 could just be repurposed, and economic relief could be efficiently distributed. In this sense, political and economic efficiency conflicted with the symbolic depth of the social realities in which they were intended to help.

Structured differently, the result *could have* been mitigation of disaster that took on a healing, revitalizing, or rejuvenating tone. Instead, requiring the symbolic action of destroying the failed crops composed the aid in a key that sounded to its participants more callously indifferent or even malevolent than solidary. The meaning of the fields may have been primarily economic to those working politically to mitigate the disaster, but their meaning to those who worked them ran far deeper, and that meaning could not easily be shed or made shallower. The fields to be plowed under did not just "stand for" or "represent" something; they—and the actions of plowing them under—spoke a social reality into life.

In focusing on this account, I am not trying to overdramatize the events; certainly if it were a matter of which social realities are harshest, far more poignant examples could be named. There is no overdramatization needed. My point is that what is at stake in this and innumerable other stories of social-ethical misfires is our very ability to understand one another and thereby to live together, work with one another, and ultimately love one another in the fullness of social reality that speaks

---

4. The Zero-92 program had originated in the 1980s as a way to minimize farm surpluses and the government costs associated with their storage and related loan forfeitures. See Ward Sinclair, "Melcher to Fight 'Zero-92' in Senate," *Washington Post*, September 20, 1987, https://www.washingtonpost.com/archive/politics/1987/09/20/melcher-to-fight-zero-92-in-senate/29a06ad5-7fb1-4449-b3fe-53caba755a81/.

us into existence. In the forming, reforming, and embodiment of social structures, the work of reading the symbols we write is essential.

In a sense, this project draws from a long line of theological reflection on the connections between liturgy and ethics, but where many foundational works in this theological space have focused on either (1) demonstrating and/or modeling how liturgy and ethics mutually inform[5] or (2) drawing implications from the liturgy-ethics relationship for applied theological questions,[6] this project maintains that liturgy and social ethics are more than dialogue partners. They share a common depth that finds its root in symbolized language and mediation. Reducing either space to ideas, concepts, commitments, or even practices tends to miss this depth. Some recent work has gestured in this direction,[7] but even as such work has emphasized the role of ritual and symbol in fields like political theology (especially in the sense of liturgy reordering bodies in ways that challenge how they are politically or socially ordered), scant attention has been given to how to *read* the realm of symbol in nonliturgical space in the first place. The field of

5. The classic example here would be the work of Louis-Marie Chauvet, in his book *Symbol and Sacrament: A Sacramental Reinterpretation of Christian Existence* (Liturgical Press, 1995). However, the heritage of the North American Liturgical Movement (beginning with the work of Virgil Michel, OSB) has borne and continues to bear significant insight into how liturgy and ethics relate. See, for example, the writing of Don Saliers (especially his *Worship as Theology: Foretaste of Glory Divine* [Abingdon, 1994]) and Bruce Morrill (especially his *Practical Sacramental Theology: At the Intersection of Liturgy and Ethics* [Cascade, 2021]), among others.

6. Some poignant examples have been the work of M. Shawn Copeland in relation to race and theological anthropology (esp. chap. 5 of her *Enfleshing Freedom: Body, Race, and Being* [Fortress, 2010]), Traci C. West in relation to social ethics (see chapter 4 of her *Disruptive Christian Ethics: When Racism and Women's Lives Matter* [Westminster John Knox, 2006]), or Timothy Brunk in relation to consumerism (see his *The Sacraments and Consumer Culture* [Liturgical Press, 2020]).

7. William Cavanaugh, for example, focuses his reflections on how liturgy and political realities both shape social reality by organizing and reorganizing bodies (see his *Torture and Eucharist: Theology, Politics, and the Body of Christ* [Blackwell, 1998]), and his work has inspired others to move in this direction (see, for example, Emmanuel Katongole, "'A Blood Thicker than the Blood of Tribalism': Eucharist and Identity in African Politics," *Modern Theology* 30, no. 2 [2014]: 319–325).

ritual studies also brings considerable wisdom to this discussion,[8] but symbol and ritual are not identical, nor is their relationship limited to symbol inhabiting ritual space (even ritual space broadly understood). Rather, this project argues that symbol is a kind of bedrock under the soil of social reality, and accurately reading its contours is a prerequisite to crafting social ethics in a just, humane, loving way.

In this light, the project is an effort to plumb the depth of how symbol speaks social reality into being and how the symbolic order animates social structures, perceptions, emotions, and values. However, doing this work in the theoretical rather than in relation to the practical would be a mistake. Instead, I have been led to this project through a struggle to make sense of political, social, and religious inertia as it manifests in experiences and accounts of a segment of contexts that is dear to me and is a central part of my identity: rural and small-town areas of the United States.[9] As such, this project proceeds by centering that particular set of social contexts, not simply because I am a product of rural and small-town America and find value in its flourishing (though that is true) but because these are contexts in which the interplay among symbol, identity, and social construction has played a constitutive (and relatively legible) role in the self-understandings of the communities that make them up.

---

8. See, for example, Catherine Bell, *Ritual Theory, Ritual Practice* (Oxford University, 2009), esp. chapters 2 and 3, and also Catherine Bell, *Ritual: Perspectives and Dimensions* (Oxford University, 1997). A helpful cartography of ritual studies can also be found in Ronald L. Grimes, *The Craft of Ritual Studies* (Oxford University, 2014).

9. To be transparent about my own social location, I have lived most of my life in rural and small-town America (specifically Minnesota), and I currently reside in Avon, Minnesota (population 1,608). My current house faces a cornfield across the street that is farmed by the dairy just down the road, and I carry with me formative memories of helping on my grandparents' dairy farm in my youth—a farm that is still in our family, though much of its land is now rented to a neighboring farmer. All this is to say that I am not unbiased in what I write here; rural is where I come from and who I am, and although I now teach at a university whose student body appears to be made up of fewer and fewer rural students, the personal stake I have in the issues I am trying to raise in this project is high.

A word more may be warranted about why it is worthwhile to center a conversation about symbol and social ethics in the social contexts of rural and small-town America. As I have pointed out elsewhere,[10] there are at least two reasons rural and small-town America merits serious theological attention. First, rural counties in the United States have, for years now, overwhelmingly voted toward the political right.[11] Consequently, social ethics (theological or not) tends to be crafted and received in significant relation to embodying and/or resisting the vocabulary of the political right for many who live in rural and small-town America. This does *not* mean that the vast majority of rural and small-town Americans actually place themselves far to the political right (though in some contexts that may be true), but it does mean that the political power—and consequently the social-ethical bent—of rural and small-town America is largely held by a single, right-leaning political party. This reality is not new, but it has been becoming consistently more pronounced, driving the rural and nonrural parts of the United States politically and socially further apart from each other.[12] It is nearly a cliché at this point to talk about the "rural-urban divide," but when the political makeup of rural areas trends so consistently in a single political direction, it would be difficult to overstate the effects this has on the social-ethical makeup of the United States, both rural and nonrural. Any time a politically powerful bloc leans extensively in a single political direction, it deserves serious social-ethical study, and rural counties are

10. See Benjamin Durheim, "Anger and Hope in Rural American Liturgy," *Religions* 13 (2022): 590, https://doi.org/10.3390/rel13070590.

11. See, for example, August Benzow, "Rural America Is Not All Trump Country: A Closer Look at the Rural Counties That Biden Won," *Economic Innovation Group*, November 17, 2020, https://eig.org/rural-america-is-not-all-trump-country/, or Don E. Albrecht, "Donald Trump and Changing Rural/Urban Voting Patterns," *Journal of Rural Studies* 91 (2022): 148–156, https://doi.org/10.1016/j.jrurstud.2022.03.009.

12. See James G. Gimpel et al., "The Urban-Rural Gulf in American Political Behavior," *Political Behavior* 42 (2020): 1343–1368, https://doi.org/10.1007/s11109-020-09601-w.

certainly that in the United States, with power protected by the makeup of structures like the electoral college and the Senate.[13]

One might ask, if rural and nonrural areas of the United States are so politically divided from each other,[14] why does this project concern itself almost exclusively with the rural side of that divide? In one sense, this is due to the fact that a very large percentage of rural Americans identify as Christian (73–83 percent, depending on the specific category of rural America),[15] and this project is primarily theological. In another sense, though, the social self-understanding of rural and small-town America lends itself particularly well to a study of symbol's role in social ethics. This is the second reason rural and small-town America merits serious theological attention: Much of the social makeup of rural and small-town America is organized into what Robert Wuthnow (drawing from Émile Durkheim) has called "moral communities."[16] While this concept may include a number of facets, the moral community is, principally, "a place to which and in which people feel an obligation to one another and to uphold the local ways of being that govern their

---

13. Emily Badger summarizes this well in her brief article "As American as Apple Pie? The Rural Vote's Disproportionate Slice of Power," *New York Times*, November 20, 2016, https://www.nytimes.com/2016/11/21/upshot/as-american-as-apple-pie-the-rural-votes-disproportionate-slice-of-power.html.

14. Even this notion of a "divide" has been the subject of significant discussion, including attempts to recast or nuance it in ways that do not pit rural and nonrural areas against one another. See, for example, Lisa Pruitt, "Mending the Rural-Urban Rift" (Presentation, Westminster Town Hall Forum, Minneapolis, Minnesota, October 25, 2022), https://westminsterforum.org/forum/mending-the-rural-urban-rift/?fbclid=IwAR1kvnc9JPA4jjgGYC-8RXY-XWUHtSIyZC5hko0EMxNA3xvj9snx0zKf7QA.

15. Public Religion Research Institute and American Communities Project Staff, "Religious Stereotypes vs. Reality in Urban, Suburban, and Rural America," *American Communities Project*, April 15, 2022, https://www.americancommunities.org/religious-stereotypes-vs-reality-in-urban-suburban-and-rural-america/#:~:text=Rural%20and%20Working%20Class%20Country,and%2083%25%20of%20Evangelical%20Hubs.

16. See Robert Wuthnow, *The Left Behind: Decline and Rage in Small-Town America* (Princeton University, 2018).

expectations about ordinary life and support their feelings of being at home and doing the right things."[17] The social context of the moral community, then, is one of readable borders defined by where and to whom one feels obligation, an affective element that has been historically mediated by land and locality (in many forms—linguistic, cultural, religious, professional, among others) in rural and small-town America.

This formative role of the local in rural self-understanding provides an exemplary vantage point from which to view how symbol grounds social reality because symbols themselves resist universalization. The potency of a symbol rests directly on its contextualization, and its meaning is defined within—rather than added onto—that social milieu.[18] In this sense, symbols are both spoken by residents of their context and also speak that context into reality in and under its residents. The primacy of locality in self-understandings of rural contexts in the United States helps unveil how symbolization operates there. To know a rural context is to know a *particular* rural context, and to know a symbol is to know a *particular* symbol or system of symbols within a context. Consequently, to speak about "the rural" or even "rural America" in general is often a fraught venture. As Allen T. Stanton points out, "One can speak about national trends, but the local stories of each community will tell a more accurate, complex, and beautiful story . . . there is no such thing as a stereotypical rural community."[19]

This resistance to universalization is exactly why the rural is illuminative for understanding symbol and social ethics. The dissonance between rural and nonrural areas of the United States is not reducible to finding a kind of discourse that everyone finds acceptable, though that

17. Wuthnow, *The Left Behind*, 4.

18. In this light, contextual methodologies are very helpful in understanding symbol and symbolization in relation to theology and ethics. For a fuller discussion of contextual approaches to theology, see Stephen B. Bevans, *Models of Contextual Theology* (Orbis, 2009).

19. Allen T. Stanton, *Reclaiming Rural: Building Thriving Rural Congregations* (Rowman and Littlefield, 2021), 16.

has not stopped some from trying to do exactly this.[20] Such a style of discourse may or may not be feasible across rural and nonrural contexts, but what certainly does manifest in engaging the moral communities of rural and small-town America is the symbolic depth of the social reality there, and thus far theological social ethics is inadequately literate in both reading and speaking to that symbolic depth. Further, what comes of increasing literacy with regard to symbols and symbolization is *not* an ability to read the same or similar symbols across social contexts; it is instead the ability to accurately *recognize*, and then read, the depth of the symbolic order in the social makeup of particular contexts. And for contexts that have often felt misunderstood, mischaracterized, and dismissed by centers of social and political power—about as universal of an experience as one is likely to find in rural areas of the United States[21]—developing a social understanding that is inclusive of the symbolic order in those contexts is a harvest that is ripe indeed. It is not enough to speak words and build social structures that are understandable on the level of simply exchanging information or that can be read as ethical from only one coherent point of view. Every linguistic expression and embodiment of social structure speaks a multiplicity of meanings into existence, meanings that are received, negotiated, and redefined in and through the relationships that constitute the communities in which they find voice. Developing and maintaining a capacity to read multiple of these meanings—to say nothing of playing a part in writing them—is a necessary task for social ethics, for liturgical theology, for pastoral ministry, and ultimately for the exercise of Christian love.

---

20. See, for example, Pruitt, "Mending the Rural-Urban Rift," or Hannah Love and Tracy Hadden Loh, "The 'Rural-Urban Divide' Furthers Myths About Race and Poverty—Concealing Effective Policy Solutions," Brookings Institution, December 8, 2020, https://www.brookings.edu/blog/the-avenue/2020/12/08/the-rural-urban-divide-furthers-myths-about-race-and-poverty-concealing-effective-policy-solutions/.

21. See, for example, Deborah Fitzgerald, *Every Farm a Factory: The Industrial Ideal in American Agriculture* (Yale University, 2003); Loka Ashwood, *For-Profit Democracy: Why the Government Is Losing the Trust of Rural America* (Yale University, 2018), or Katherine J. Cramer, *The Politics of Resentment: Rural Consciousness in Wisconsin and the Rise of Scott Walker* (University of Chicago, 2016).

In order to undertake this work, this project unfolds in six chapters. The first chapter focuses on conceptualizing social realities in rural and small-town areas of the United States (in addition to addressing the difficulty of defining "rural" in the first place),[22] examining common narratives that distinguish rural social reality from the nonrural and narratives that tend to be held in common between rural and nonrural areas of the United States. In both cases, the focus on the locality of rural communities plays an essential role, whether in contradistinction to the perceived separation from nonrural centers of power or in resonant factors that affect both nonrural and rural contexts. In rural moral communities, the knowing of one's neighbors—those who live in physically proximate spaces—precipitates both a blessing and a burden for social life. In contexts where "everybody knows everybody,"[23] problems in one area may easily lead to problems in other areas. One might think of the social fabric of the moral community as one-ply; if it tears, it tears all the way through, which plays a part in how many rural and small-town residents conceive of (and sometimes avoid) conflict. The rural moral community navigates symbolization and social ethics without much of a safety net or room for missteps.

The second chapter serves to provide a conceptual bridge between the rural as moral community and reading the role of symbolization in its social makeup. To forge this bridge, the chapter scaffolds around critical realist sociology, especially as it appears in the work of Margaret Archer, and around the ritual studies work of Catherine Bell. Critical realist sociology has recently been used to understand social structures theologically,[24] but its further value as a theoretical lens through which to study symbol and social ethics derives from at least three of its characteristics: First, critical realist sociology includes an earnest respect for the unpredictability and even wildness of social structures as they

22. Stanton, *Reclaiming Rural*, 2–5.

23. See Wuthnow, *The Left Behind*, 31–38.

24. See Daniel Finn, "What Is a Sinful Social Structure?" *Theological Studies* 77, no. 1 (2016): 136–164.

develop in relation to social actions and changes. Second, it is unshy about confessing the reality of structures and relationships that build them, which can be an important corrective against any temptation to reduce social meaning simply to perception. Third, critical realist social theory accounts well for the interplay between individual and communal agency, a relationship that is fundamental to understanding how rural moral communities often act and develop.

Catherine Bell's work in ritual studies provides, among other gifts, a framework for understanding social realities that are intentionally symbolic. This is, of course, not the only subject of her work, but the project juxtaposes this aspect of Bell's work alongside Archer's theory in order to help translate between critical realist social theory and liturgical/sacramental understandings of the symbolic order (the subject of chapter 3). When understanding the depth of symbolism is a conscious or intentional goal, the work of doing so also produces tools for reading symbols in contexts where such work is implicit or unintentional. Developing an ability to use these tools aids in guarding against an impulse that seems to be quite commonplace in American society (at least among my own students and conversation partners): an impulse to regard as false or mischaracterized any symbolism that did not immediately appear as obvious to the person in question. Examples of this impulse include everything from resistance that many white persons can display to "making something about race that really isn't about race"[25] to offense that persons can take in response to being informed that certain of their words or actions are microaggressive or simply offensive. What something is "really about" is a question that is mediated in large part by the symbolic order—not as a mode of representing meaning but as a mode of *embodying* meaning—and ritual studies can provide ways to engage that modality.

In the third chapter, the project turns to the ways contemporary liturgical and sacramental theologies have understood symbol and the

25. Eduardo Bonilla-Silva's work is instructive in this regard; see his *Racism Without Racists: Color-Blind Racism and the Persistence of Racial Inequality in America*, 6th ed. (Rowman and Littlefield, 2022).

symbolic order. Symbol has long been acknowledged as an essential concept through which to understand liturgy, but work on symbol and social ethics is far less common. At least partially responsible for this lacuna is a multiplicity of understandings of symbol that make their way into scholarly and popular reflection. For example, when contemporary liturgical/sacramental theologians do sustained work on symbol, they often employ a definition of symbol (or of the symbolic order) that derives from the work of Louis-Marie Chauvet and the theologies in conversation with his thought, or perhaps Karl Rahner's work on symbol, or other theological sources. When work in theological social ethics taps the concept of symbol (something done far less often than in liturgical/sacramental theology), it tends to do so in conversation with sociological or philosophical understandings of symbol, like those operative in Émile Durkheim or Paul Ricœur.[26] At other times, theological sources will use symbol as a supporting concept without sustained reflection on what the symbolic order is and how it may operate.[27] This diversity of thought and method is not necessarily a bad thing, but the way many liturgical-theological sources have come to understand the concept of symbol rests on creative theological work that has moved, in conversation with philosophical and sociological sources, beyond the definition of symbol that those sources assume. Generally speaking, theological conceptualizations of symbol have moved further and further away from viewing the symbol as representation, image, or reference point[28] and more toward understanding the symbol as mediation, as a making present, as a kind of making real.

---

26. See, for example, William A. Stahl, "Symbols and Ethics: An Approach to the Civil Religion Debate," *Union Seminary Quarterly Review* 34, no. 4 (1979): 229–238; Marieke Maes, "Paul Ricœr: Symbols of Good and Evil in History, the Bible, and in Our Time," *European Journal for Philosophy of Religion* 12, no. 4 (2020): 161–174; or Kenneth Vaux, "Law and Lamb: AKEDAH and the Search for a Deep Religious Symbol for an Ecumenical Bioethics," *Christian Bioethics* 5, no. 3 (1999): 213–219.

27. See, for example, Nichole M. Flores, *The Aesthetics of Solidarity: Our Lady of Guadalupe and American Democracy* (Georgetown University, 2021), whose thought provides a framework for chap. 4 of this book.

28. This has been true outside liturgical/sacramental theology as well. See, for example, Roger Haight, *Jesus Symbol of God* (Orbis, 2000).

Understanding the symbol from the vantage point of liturgical/sacramental theology allows for a "reading" of social realities embodied in their structural and cultural components that resists reducing the meaning of those realities to one's own experience, perception, and judgment thereof. Such reduction can be especially problematic when applied inductively, that is, reducing the depth of meaning suffused through a broad social reality to a one-dimensional image derived from a perception or experience in relation to one piece of that reality. For example, Stanton has argued convincingly that two competing narratives tend to hold sway in common perceptions of rural American life: one as "agrarian paradise" and the other as "rural decay."[29] In Stanton's words, "When people describe rural communities, they tend to offer one of two narratives. The first is popular within theological circles, placing an emphasis on agrarianism, often using the terms 'agrarian' and 'rural' interchangeably . . . The second narrative and perhaps the more popular of the two, paints rural communities as places of inevitable decline. Propelled by books like JD Vance's *Hillbilly Elegy*, these narratives skew data to show that rural communities will inevitably collapse."[30]

Both narratives miss the complexity of life in rural areas of the United States, but that recognition on its own is not enough to help read the complexity that one would otherwise miss. Put differently, to know better is not necessarily to do better. Instead, a capacity for reading multiple layers of meaning, mediated by symbols, is necessary to carry an adequate—that is not to say *accurate*—view of rural social reality. That capacity finds a privileged place in Christian liturgical and sacramental practices, as well as in theological approaches to them. Reading and writing symbol takes more than understanding; it takes practice.

Having laid out theoretical foundations as they find expression in rural contexts of the United States, chapters 4–6 turn to reading the symbolic order in particular social realities in rural and small-town America. Chapter 4 begins this work by reading what may be called a

29. Stanton, *Reclaiming Rural*, 5, 9.

30. Stanton, *Reclaiming Rural*, 2.

"rural aesthetic," particularly as it relates to perceptions of solidarity in rural areas of the United States. The work of Nichole Flores provides the central lens through which to read this interplay of aesthetics and solidarity. Many rural residents—both those represented in the literature and those whom I've interviewed in the course of ethnographic and qualitative research—speak of desirable aspects of social life in similar ways. Knowing everyone (or the vast majority of people) in a community and sharing similar beliefs, appreciation of the natural world and its nearness, independence that is communally conditioned, trust in relative local safety, and a number of other components tend to make up this rural aesthetic.[31] This aesthetic conditions and is conditioned by what Katherine J. Cramer calls "rural consciousness,"[32] a perspective that tends to value the local in most things and often harbors a suspicion of social and political powers beyond the local. In such an aesthetic, priority is generally given to practicing solidarity with those geographically close or close in family or social relationship.[33] In some ways, this simply means that rural solidarity is conditioned significantly by subsidiarity, and in others it means that responding to what ethics may require is primarily thought of as a local endeavor, and one goes beyond the local only in cases of significant need. In all cases, however, symbol builds and sustains this rural aesthetic.

Symbols, of course, are never ethically neutral. Some symbolic systems serve to build up community relationships, solidarity, justice, and love, while other symbolic systems serve to privilege only certain groups of persons, oppress others, or sow discord and division. Often the same

31. The role of churches in this rural sensibility is well-documented. See, for example, Michael Adam Beck and Tyler Kleeberger, *Fresh Expressions of the Rural Church* (Abingdon, 2022).

32. Cramer, *The Politics of Resentment*, 45–111.

33. For a discussion of strengthening these and other small-town characteristics, see Andy Stanton-Henry, *Recovering Abundance: Twelve Practices for Small-Town Leaders* (Fortress, 2022), or Norman Wirzba, *Agrarian Spirit: Cultivating Faith, Community, and the Land* (University of Notre Dame, 2022).

system of symbols embodies a mixture of both healthy and unhealthy social realities. Chapter 5 focuses attention on the relationship between symbolization and social sin, especially as it tends to live in rural and small-town America. In this the work of Daniel Daly on social structures is illuminative, helping to use critical realist sociology to bridge between social theory and social ethics. The chapter then explores a number of examples of social or structural sin as they have unfolded in rural contexts, maintaining that symbolization is just as much at work in vicious structures and practices as in virtuous ones.

In the sixth chapter, the project turns to a social reality whose symbolic depth has become significantly threatening to the vitality of the rural moral community and its aesthetic: the rise of understanding community as increasingly (or in some cases primarily) virtual. Virtual community—mediated overwhelmingly in online space through everything from social media to shopping and financial services to education and entertainment—carries at its core the reversal of a primary attribute of the rural moral community, namely, that the moral community is defined by locality. Excising this characteristic from the rural moral community changes the nature of the community in at least two ways that bear on our discussion: First, it diffuses the obligation inherent to the moral community across vast virtual space, severely diluting it on both the virtual and local levels, and second, it performs a fallacy that we are free to choose not only which moral communities we inhabit but also which particular aspects of those communities we embody or reject. Additionally, symbols can become more fluid in virtual space, but they tend to do so by becoming decontextualized, and while in a local moral community, a de-contextualized symbol tends to *lose* meaning, virtual space is incredibly efficient at allowing users to substitute their own contexts or perceptions of context for symbols and speech, which confuses and changes symbolic meaning rather than emptying it. Chapter 6 is an effort to reckon with the telecommunication of symbols—particularly as they carry political and religious meaning.

Altogether, lessons taken from liturgical and sacramental theology can provide social ethics with an acuity—with a literacy—that it otherwise may lack. This is not exactly a *new* way of doing social ethics; it is a way of seeing more deeply what social-ethical action and study *already do*. In being able to reckon more readily with the symbolic depth of social reality both inside and outside ritual, we are better positioned to engage both the depth of individual relationships and the full meaning and reality of more structured relationships among social, political, and religious communities. In a word, we may be better able to build structures that help us love.

I

Theory in a Rural Key

CHAPTER ONE

What Is "Rural"?

Introduction: The Difficulty of a Definition

SEVERAL YEARS AGO, I was teaching a course on rural ministry and theology, and the class was blessed with a wealth of students from around the globe, many of whom had some experience of rural areas in their home countries. The course itself had mostly focused on issues associated with practicing ministry in rural and small-town contexts of the United States, and while that didn't necessarily present a problem (many of the students would be entering ministry in the United States), it did provide plenty of opportunities for discussing what constitutes "rural" in different settings. In one class session close to midterm, we were discussing food and grocery store access in rural areas of the United States. The discussion turned to issues of travel time, food deserts, and related challenges that ironically are relatively common in some of the most agriculturally active areas of the United States.[1] As we collectively wrestled with food accessibility in rural America, one priest in the class, who was from Haiti, dryly noted, "I don't really understand what you mean by *rural*; your rural has refrigeration!" His comment was a helpful moment of reorienting perspective, but more than that, it pointed to a common difficulty in any attempt to speak truths about rural America and "the rural" more generally: They tend to resist easy and clear definition, often instead operating as products of assumption, conjecture, or simply ideals that become fuzzier the closer one examines them.

A definition of the rural might seem relatively straightforward to craft. However, even those bodies that actually require a strict,

1. See, for example, Lois Wright Morton and Troy C. Blanchard, "Starved for Access: Life in Rural America's Food Deserts," *Rural Realities* 1, no. 4 (2007): 1–10.

measurable definition of the rural tend to have a multiplicity of ways to define it. For example, the US Census Bureau defines *rural* as any area that is not urban, *urban* being defined in the bureau's view (for the 2020 census at least) as any area with a "densely settled core of census blocks" that includes at least 2,000 units or a population of 5,000.[2] Anything with population or housing units less than that is rural. Previously, for the 2010 census, the Census Bureau had defined urban as an area with 2,500 people or more, and at that time, the Office of Management and Budget (OMB) defined the rural as any area with an urban core of fewer than 50,000 people,[3] rather a broad difference. The OMB has further clarified that it defines metropolitan counties (counties that are not rural) as inclusive of "outlying counties," defined as those for whom at least 25 percent of the resident labor force commutes to a nearby urban center.[4] Again, rural counties are any that don't fall into these definitions. The US Department of Agriculture's Economic Research Service, for its part, largely uses the Census Bureau's data along with the OMB to delineate among (1) open countryside, (2) rural towns—those with fewer than 2,000 housing units or a population of less than 5,000, and (3) urban and metropolitan areas with more population and/or density than this.[5]

This brief glimpse into governmental definitions of the rural points to a common problem in defining the space: While there is a nearly constant, universal sense that the rural is that space with "fewer people," the question of exactly how few, and by what metrics to measure that few,

---

2. US Census Bureau, "Urban and Rural," accessed March 18, 2025, https://www.census.gov/programs-surveys/geography/guidance/geo-areas/urban-rural.html.

3. US Health Resources and Services Administration, "How We Define Rural," accessed March 18, 2025, https://www.hrsa.gov/rural-health/about-us/what-is-rural.

4. US Department of Agriculture Economic Research Service, "What Is Rural?," updated January 8, 2025, https://www.ers.usda.gov/topics/rural-economy-population/rural-classifications/what-is-rural/.

5. US Department of Agriculture Economic Research Service, "Rural Classifications: Overview," updated January 8, 2025, https://www.ers.usda.gov/topics/rural-economy-population/rural-classifications/.

yields answers that are anything but universal and constant. The lack of a clear popular definition of the rural, however, does not appear to lead to widespread agnosticism regarding what the rural is; I've never been in a conversation with a person who, when the subject of rural life comes up, pauses the conversation to ask what *rural* means or to clarify how I'm using the word. Instead, most people tend to do with the rural what we do with so many other hazily definable concepts: We substitute the related narratives, myths, experiences, and snippets of perspectives that we have at our disposal for the definition of the concept itself. What the rural is, then, in the minds of many I've spoken with (both students and the rural persons I've had the opportunity to interview in my research), becomes a pastiche of ideas and understandings that layer upon one another—sometimes resonating and other times contradicting—an amalgam produced by a cacophony of voices each speaking "rural."

At times, these sometimes competing, sometimes resonating narratives can be pulled together into larger composite strains of perspectives, as Allen T. Stanton does in his book *Reclaiming Rural*.[6] Stanton argues that there are two central (and opposing) narratives that strive to hold sway in the American imagination of the rural: the rural as an idyllic country paradise synonymous with agrarian living and the rural as a decaying social apparatus bound for collapse.[7] Stanton's point is not to pick one or the other or even simply to correct them both, though he does provide essential nuance through which to understand the narratives and critique their accuracy. His emphasis is on the ways these narratives take on expression in both rural and nonrural life. He speaks of Wendell Berry's works as providing proof texts of rural agrarian virtue and cohesion for those who wish only a surface-level engagement of rural reality and of J. D. Vance's *Hillbilly Elegy* reembodying in the American perspective the old idea that the rural is of its own fault poor, culturally backward, and in decline.[8] He adds to this

6. Stanton, *Reclaiming Rural*, especially the introduction and chap. 1.

7. Stanton, *Reclaiming Rural*, 5–15.

8. Stanton, *Reclaiming Rural*, 8, 10.

his own experiences of the rural and the ways in which it both expresses some of the constitutive structure of the narratives—he says his childhood home community "was a picturesque embodiment of Wendell Berry's ideal community" and also conversely tells of carrying his rural identity through higher education as "a mark against me and my future success"[9]—and additionally challenges them. He notes both that the Ku Klux Klan was founded in his home community and that studies have shown "rural communities have a greater potential for economic mobility than metropolitan areas."[10] The rural is complex in Stanton's perspective, not simply because it is multifaceted—though it certainly is that—but also because discordant narratives live and operate side by side in America's understanding of its rural self.

Stanton's articulation of two competing narratives that form how rural America is understood is helpful, but he is hardly the only one to have articulated defining narratives of rural American life. Numerous other authors have also done so, and my goal in this chapter is to pull together a representative snapshot of that pastiche of rural American narratives. The foundational methodological conviction of the chapter is that to best understand rural America, one should be prepared to work contextually, that is, to take into account not simply rural space or demographics or politics or labor but to approach all these and the narratives that undergird them in order to see the rural for what it is. To do so will yield a diversity of images, not all of which can be easily harmonized into a cohesive whole but which nevertheless layer upon one another to form a thing that is both real and distinct from the nonrural. One need not (must not) smelt all narratives of the rural together into a single metanarrative. Rather, we should listen in each narrative for truth that speaks there. Such is the aim of this chapter: to give the rest of this book an accurate (though certainly not exhaustive) approximation of the social reality that is its subject. To do so, the chapter attends first to a set of narratives that emphasizes the distinctiveness or differences

9. Stanton, *Reclaiming Rural*, 7, 11.

10. Stanton, *Reclaiming Rural*, 9, 13.

between rural and nonrural social contexts and then moves to a set of narratives that emphasizes the shared influences and realities that transcend any American rural-nonrural divide. The chapter then culminates in examining the role of narrative and tradition in forming and reforming an understanding of American rural life and context and the ways they open our conversation to the operation of social structure, ritual, symbol, and social ethics.

Narratives of Distinctiveness: Moral Community

To begin, a word may be warranted about what I mean by *narratives of distinctiveness*. By this, I do not mean to suggest that these narratives of the rural paint it as wholly different from or utterly alien to nonrural contexts. Rather, to be distinct is to embody particular emphases of characteristics that distinguish one reality from another. For example, a distinctive characteristic of the blue jay species of birds is its blue plumage, but many other birds have blue feathers as well (the tree swallow, white-breasted nuthatch, belted kingfisher, etc.). This doesn't mean that the blue jay somehow owns blue or has the most blue, or the best blue, or the only blue. It means that if one is going to describe the blue jay, it's probably a good idea to mention that it's got blue feathers, even if it does not boast exclusive rights to blueness. Likewise, in speaking of distinctive characteristics of rural America, I do not mean to challenge the idea that many of these characteristics are also present in various ways in nonrural contexts of the United States. Of course they are. However, to accurately describe rural America, these distinctive characteristics are essential to note.

With this caveat in mind, one central narrative for understanding rural America is that rural social reality is inseparable from the social reality of the American small town, conceived of as a moral community. The core principle of this narrative is that to understand rural spaces and contexts, one needs to disabuse oneself of an image of human community that conceptually prioritizes individual identity and self-determination apart from community influences and content. In a word, this narrative maintains that individualism is a secondary rather than a primary operative anthropological construct in rural American contexts. Much can be and has been said about American individualism,[11] but as the rural sociologist Robert Wuthnow points out, people who inhabit the rural contexts of the United States "*may be* rugged individualists. But they are not fundamentally that. Spend some time in rural America and you realize one thing: people there are community-oriented."[12] In this view, to understand rural contexts of the United States is to understand not simply the rural itself. It is also to understand the rural as organized into and around small-town communities whose identities Wuthnow describes, drawing from Émile Durkheim's work and the authors that follow in his intellectual tradition, as moral communities.[13]

For Wuthnow, a moral community is a social construction, not an ethical one. A moral community is "a place to which and in which people feel an obligation to one another and to uphold the local ways of being that govern their expectations about ordinary life and support their feelings of being at home and doing the right things."[14] In Wuthnow's perspective, the rural moral community (read: small town) is both an arbiter of social authority—in terms of setting the stage for what "ordinary life" is and reasonable expectations surrounding it—and a constitutive mediator of identity that operates through personal obligations to both local customs and local persons (neighbors).[15] Of course, understanding moral community in this way requires members of a moral community to actually *know* both the local customs and some

11. And this has been going on for some time, particularly in theological circles. See especially the seminal work of Virgil Michel, OSB, for example, his *Christian Social Reconstruction* (Bruce Publishing, 1937). Outside theology, see the classic work of Robert D. Putnam, *Bowling Alone: The Collapse and Revival of American Community* (Simon and Schuster, 2000).

12. Wuthnow, *The Left Behind*, 4. Emphasis in original.

13. Wuthnow, *The Left Behind*, 4.

14. Wuthnow, *The Left Behind*, 4.

15. Wuthnow, *The Left Behind*, 14–15.

significant number of local persons—a requirement that can take a good many years to satisfy. When I speak about life in a small community or rural area, and particularly when I'm speaking *in* a small town or rural area, I often mention as kind of a throwaway line that if all goes well, it can take about two generations, or forty years, to become a "local" in a small town. If all does not go well (for reasons of injustice or prejudice or anything else), that timeframe can be rather longer. Thus far, no rural residents have corrected me; instead, when I say that, the room tends to fill with knowing nods, wry smiles, and stories about formative experiences of becoming "local." In Wuthnow's research, he reports that "many of the people who lived in their communities for less than two decades said they still didn't feel like they quite belonged."[16]

The length of time it can take to become local is one reason qualitative and ethnographic research methods have been so successful in studying rural social contexts. In a rural moral community, stories live a long time, and as they live, they grow into the bones of the social authority that is that moral community. Knowing these stories, and being a part of them, inculcates in community members a sense of who "we" are and how "we" live. Because this "we" is constituted also by mutual relationships of obligation and support, this "we" of the moral community is also the primary location of social trust. External bodies that conduct studies can have a difficult time accessing this "we," unless they are able to do so by sustained engagement and frank, personal connection (not always easy to come by in large quantitative research efforts). As Katherine J. Cramer notes in relation to her research in rural Wisconsin, "I got to know people. I spent time in their barns, at their favorite hang-outs, in their chairs. They asked to see pictures of my daughter, and I asked to see pictures of their families in return. I got manure on my toes. I got insulted, and I got and gave hugs,"[17] and in the end, "I learned that, rather than obscure who I am, I had to be a

16. Wuthnow, *The Left Behind*, 29.

17. Cramer, *The Politics of Resentment*, 28–29.

human being in order to be welcomed into their conversations."[18] This is part of what it means to engage rural social reality as moral communities; access to truths of those realities can often be gated behind the requirement to engage on a human, personal level.

Cramer's experience resonates with my own primary research. In 2022 and 2023, I collaborated with two undergraduate students to conduct qualitative research in six rural Christian congregations.[19] To be clear, I am not a formally trained sociologist or political scientist, but I carry a deep conviction that to do theology well, particularly theology in a contextual mode, requires primary engagement of relevant social contexts as well as secondary research related to it. My own personal history and social location are rural, but my perspective is buttressed by primary research in rural Christianity in conversation with the more significant work done by rural sociologists and others in related fields. In this, I do not mean to dismiss quantitative or other research methods or to give in to the "ethnographic fallacy" (a mistake of "taking too much from the particular without contextualization");[20] it's just that often in the case of the rural United States, the particular rural moral community *is* the relevant contextualization.

This work in rural Christianity provides the background for many parts of this book,[21] and I bring it up now because in the 2022 research, it became clear that to engage rural Christian understandings of their

18. Cramer, *The Politics of Resentment*, 32.

19. These two students were Lydia Mattern in 2022 for the project "Anger and Hope in Rural Christianity" and Gilbert Perez in 2023 for the project "Symbol and Social Ethics in Rural Christianity."

20. This definition of the ethnographic fallacy comes from Ashwood (*For-Profit Democracy: Why the Government Is Losing the Trust of Rural America*, 233), but it was initially coined by Stephen Steinberg (quoted in Mitchell Duneier, *Sidewalk* [Farrar, Straus, and Giroux, 2020], 343).

21. In summer 2022, Lydia and I researched five rural Christian congregations, and in summer 2023, Gilbert and I conducted a more in-depth research project on a single rural congregation. I have intentionally kept the focus of this project broader than my own primary research because the central thesis of the discussion regarding symbol and social ethics transcends the particular communities I have engaged. As

own moral communities, it was first necessary to traverse the space between socially safe discourse about rural communities in general and the more socially intimate space of speaking about one's home moral community. The 2022 research focused on experiences and perspectives of anger and hope in rural Christian congregations, and while interviewees often readily spoke about social contexts wider than their home community, they were generally pretty leery about disclosing specific perspectives regarding their own community until they felt more familiar with their interviewers, even though we made clear that we would be anonymizing all places, names, and identifying information. For example, one interviewee claimed there wasn't any significant anger or resentment in her home community of 240, but if one included the neighboring towns of approximate populations of 3,000 and 5,000, she could name all kinds of things people were angry about.

Essentially, the social image of the moral community—a home community sustained by relationships of obligation and support—grounded the vast majority of interviews we did, even though no interviewee actually used that term. For example, when speaking to one interviewee about what is important in her social and religious life, she immediately spoke of her family relationships and the ways they interact with the local community: "I don't know how many times I hear on the way home from church 'Mom, who was that guy that came up and talked to me about fishing?' or 'Who is that guy that came up and congratulated me on my football game?' . . . and I'll say who that was, and they just, they *feel* because people know their name."[22] This affective component of social identity, of *feeling* at home and being known by the community, is an integral part of how rural moral communities operate.

That a person or group would identify with a social context in which they feel at home or a sense of belonging is certainly not unique to

such, that primary research is part of this discussion, but this discussion is concerned with more than just that.

22. Anonymized interviewee (resident of a Minnesota town of approximately two hundred people), recorded interview with Lydia Mattern, summer 2022. Emphasis in original recording.

the rural. What makes the moral community distinctive to rural social reality is its significant weight in determining individual and social identity. Local institutions like the high school and its mascot and sports, or prominent local businesses, or local landmarks known by colloquialisms rather than official names ("the old Smith place" that's been home to multiple families subsequent to the Smiths or the "Jolly Jack's building," which hasn't been Jolly Jack's in more than three decades) all function to yield a distinguishable local identity that is recognizable to those in the moral community and those who neighbor it. I still remember my father's tongue-in-cheek reaction when, after my daughter was born, I moved with my family to a small town about forty miles away from my childhood hometown: Recognizing the likelihood of cheering for his granddaughter in a rival small town's sports programs, he quipped (referencing the color of our adopted hometown's high school sports uniforms), "Well, I guess I could wear purple." In a rural moral community, the local is stamped on one's identity.

Physical locality is augmented by social practice in building and defining the moral community. Local rituals and municipal festivals are all part of this, but as Wuthnow notes, the bounds of the moral community are also continually defined by social interaction and invitation. Describing a hypothetical situation wherein you are caught in a conversation at the local post office and your discussion partner discloses that they heard your daughter is getting married, Wuthnow explains, "The appropriate response . . . is to tell your interlocutor how pleased you would be if they would come. And your interlocutor's response should be, yes, I'd like that, and is there anything I can do to help? An interaction of this kind is in small but important measure an indication of the way living in a rural community entails moral obligations."[23] The point in this hypothetical is less about who gets to attend a wedding than it is about how the moral community takes shape. To wit, membership in a moral community is not binary (as if you're strictly "in" or strictly "out"); membership can be partial, it can be more and less, and it can be healthy, unhealthy, tenuous, stalwart, constructive, toxic, and any

23. Wuthnow, *The Left Behind*, 31.

number of other modifiers. If you choose to invite your conversation partner to the wedding, that particular bond of the moral community likely strengthens, and it likely weakens if the opportunity for invitation passes without you seizing it. Action and inaction both impact one's role and membership in the moral community because, to be frank, the number of bodies in that rural moral community is by definition relatively small, so every action or inaction of every member of that moral community carries a noticeable impact on the whole social context.

The moral community is a formative narrative image of rural social reality in the United States, but it is not the only relevant one. While an understanding of the rural as self-organized into moral communities can give some insight into the importance of locality, relationship, obligation, and support for rural contexts, it tends to be a kind of structural image rather than one associated with how rural perspectives form and grow. This discussion now turns to the latter, with the goal of augmenting the structural image of the rural moral community with the image of rural consciousness.

Narratives of Distinctiveness: Rural Consciousness

The term *rural consciousness* has been used on occasion at least as early as 1940 to describe a perspectival whole that is distinguishable from urban/city ways of looking at the world.[24] Since then, it has developed in a number of ways but gained renewed prominence (and scholarly attention) following Katherine J. Cramer's seminal work *The Politics of Resentment*.[25] In *Resentment*, Cramer argues that while the rural-nonrural divide can be understood in many ways, one foundational

24. See Ernst Harms, "The Rural Consciousness," *Social Forces* 19, no. 1 (1940): 29–40.

25. Cramer, *The Politics of Resentment*. In fact, Cramer had been using the terminology of *rural consciousness* for a number of years prior to the publication of *Resentment*, but *Resentment* was the book that ignited much of the renewed attention to the concept (see Katherine Cramer Walsh, "Putting Inequality in Its Place: Rural Consciousness and the Power of Perspective," *American Political Science Review* 106, no. 3 [2012]: 517–532).

apparatus for that understanding is a discrete perspective or lens that she calls *rural consciousness.*[26] It is a hermeneutic of sorts—though she does not extensively use that term—a lens through which rural persons view their particular realities and the wider realities (social, political, etc.) of which they are a part. For Cramer, part of the problem in previous studies of rural American contexts has been, to put it bluntly, inattention to the contextual perspectives that craft rural American contexts in the first place. Demographic studies, political surveys, ethnographic research, and any number of other sources of useful information can provide a detailed picture of a context, but without attention to the perspectives of people living the context—as defined by *themselves* rather than interpreted by visitors to that context—the detailed picture can falter on close examination.[27]

Cramer's work describes a distinct root set of constitutive characteristics of a perspective that tends to be shared in rural contexts—in her case, those in Wisconsin, though she argues that Wisconsin operates as something of a microcosm of the United States more generally.[28] She argues that this rural consciousness helps contextualize much of the social and political outlook of rural folks in the United States. As Cramer describes it, rural consciousness has three parts, each of which this discussion will now briefly engage: "(1) a belief that rural areas are ignored by decision makers, including policy makers, (2) a perception that rural areas do not get their fair share of resources, and (3) a sense that rural folks have fundamentally distinct values and lifestyles, which are misunderstood and disrespected by city folks."[29]

26. Cramer, *The Politics of Resentment*, 12.

27. Cramer is not unique in this, but her work is particularly illuminative for our discussion. See also Arlie Russell Hochschild, *Strangers in Their Own Land: Anger and Mourning on the American Right* (The New Press, 2016); Cynthia M. Duncan, *Worlds Apart: Poverty and Politics in Rural America*, 2nd ed. (Yale University, 2014); and Lyn C. MacGregor, *Habits of the Heartland: Small-Town Life in Modern America* (Cornell, 2010).

28. Cramer, *The Politics of Resentment*, 210.

29. Cramer, *The Politics of Resentment*, 12.

The first pillar, if you will, of Cramer's rural consciousness—that of believing rural areas are largely ignored or swept to the side by centers of power—has both a political and an economic vein, and of course the two are deeply interrelated. In her book *For-Profit Democracy*, Loka Ashwood describes at length the ways large corporate and governmental interests have wreaked havoc on the natural and social well-being of rural residents in Burke County, Georgia.[30] Among the stories she relates is one of Patty Sutton, who raises pine trees for timber and spoke to Ashwood about the energy company that forced its power lines across Sutton's property and (in her perspective) whose negligence caused a fire that cost her thousands of dollars in crop damages. When asked if she sought compensation for the damage, Sutton responded, "My mother and I sent a letter. I didn't hear a thing back. They have the luxury of not caring about what they do wrong. They think that they are invincible, that they can do anything."[31]

Sutton's perspective, that external forces care not a whit for the rural consequences of their actions, is a common theme throughout Ashwood's text. It mirrors the political perceptions of many in Cramer's study, for whom it nearly went without saying that "politicians and government in general are tone-deaf to people outside the major cities."[32] Wuthnow, too, has noted in his study of American farmers that they held a widespread belief that whatever influence powerful agents exerted on agricultural markets "rarely involved anything farmers did or could do."[33] One might be tempted at this point to insist that such experiences of being kept outside of access to power and influence are not unique to rural folks, and that would be correct. However, Cramer notes that these rural experiences share a rootedness not in the experience itself but in a prior milieu of locality and self-perception: "This

30. Ashwood, *For-Profit Democracy*.

31. Patty Sutton, qtd. in Ashwood, *For-Profit Democracy*, 49.

32. Cramer, *The Politics of Resentment*, 60.

33. Robert Wuthnow, *In the Blood: Understanding America's Farm Families* (Princeton University, 2015), 164.

is not just alienation, or a lack of trust, or low efficacy with respect to powerful institutions. These sentiments are tightly bound to a sense of place identity. Simply put, many folks I met . . . identified as rural people and equated membership in that category with being a person who is systematically ignored and left out of the exercise of power."[34]

Within this narrative, part of being rural is by definition to be without equitable access to political or economic power. Such a narrative might seem odd to nonrural persons who may perceive rural states as setting significant portions of the national political agenda of the United States, but the question is more complex than whether rural concerns have any voice at all. We have noted earlier that certain US governmental structures exist with the idea of counteracting a possible tyranny of an urban majority—the makeup of the Senate, for example, which is not weighted by population, or the electoral college, which includes Senate seats as part of defining a state's total elector count. This does not appear to have assuaged rural American perceptions of political marginalization. Instead, rural consciousness in the United States is conditioned by a real sense that the centers of power (political, economic, or otherwise) chiefly concern themselves with their own affairs and impose ill-fitting policies on people in rural contexts, who had inadequate say in crafting them.

Closely connected with believing that rural contexts are kept largely out of political or economic circles of influence is the second pillar of Cramer's rural consciousness: a sense that resources are not equitably distributed between rural and nonrural places. This aspect of rural consciousness helps throw into relief something that is also true about political and economic power: At issue in rural consciousness is not *whether* those in rural spaces have any say or access to resources but rather whether that say, and resource access are adequate or equitable.[35] For example, many rural areas experience a significant need

34. Cramer, *The Politics of Resentment*, 66.

35. Significant energy has been invested in exploring what equitable access to and production of resources might look like in rural American contexts, but they often center, laudibly, on how to craft adequate rural responses and organizing principles/

for eldercare and hospice services. However, that need is often spread out over many miles and travel hours, meaning it is often difficult to staff sufficient eldercare and hospice offerings. In response, facilities that offer these services face difficult choices about whether to run understaffed or simply to close. Neither case is ideal, but the reality of that choice leads to rural pushback against initiatives that may seem beneficial or even common sense from a nonrural perspective, as was the case with the bipartisan opposition from rural districts and states to the federal staffing mandate initiative for nursing homes proposed by the Biden administration in 2023.[36] The point is that within political and economic systems that value density of demand in order to maximize profit and efficiency in satiating that demand, areas of low-density but nonzero demand offer precious little innate incentive to ensure adequate services.[37] Put differently, low-density need is not the same as *no* need, but when dollars and other resources are allocated by centers of power to address community needs, rural communities regularly feel shortchanged.

Related to this feeling of being shortchanged or passed over is an exacerbating sense that decisions that may seem to have a small or negligible impact in nonrural areas can wreak havoc in rural spaces. In Cramer's words, recalling a conversation with a group of rural men about school funding, "a 1 percent tax increase 'means a hell

---

actions rather than how to make the rural-nonrural relationship more equitable. See, for example, Don E. Albrecht, *Building a Resilient Twenty-First-Century Economy for Rural America* (University Press of Colorado, 2020).

36. American Health Care Association / National Center for Assisted Living, "ICYMI: Democrat Lawmaker Opposition of Federal Staffing Mandate for Nursing Homes Is Growing," November 30, 2023, https://www.ahcancal.org/News-and-Communications/Press-Releases/Pages/ICYMI-Democrat-Lawmaker-Opposition-Of-Federal-Staffing-Mandate-For-Nursing-Homes-Is-Growing.aspx#:~:text=Much%20of%20the%20opposition%20comes,with%20this%20impossible%2C%20unfunded%20mandate.

37. See, for example, Drew Brookie, "Rural Veterans and the Tyranny of Distance," U.S. Department of Agriculture, 2011, https://www.usda.gov/media/blog/2011/08/03/rural-veterans-and-tyranny-distance.

of a lot more here' than it does in the metro areas . . . In their eyes, decisions about funding for schools mean that small communities are the victims of distributive injustice."[38] Add to this the oft-maligned "unfunded mandates"[39] that can impose significant burdens on small communities whose tax revenue is often already spread quite thin, and it makes sense that rural consciousness would include the perspective that rural areas do not receive an equitable share of resources to ensure the common good.

The third aspect of rural consciousness, that rural values and lifestyles both differ from and are looked down on by nonrural folks, has both a contemporary and a historical dimension, and they are mutually informative. From a historical perspective, particularly in reference to agrarian rural lifestyles and values, nonrural values have had a troubled—and, often enough, devastating—impact on the health of rural areas and the communities that make them up. The classic example would be the development of industrialized agriculture, which pitted the rural value of small-scale and long-running family farming against a system that values massive production over community vitality. Deborah Fitzgerald documents this well in her text *Every Farm a Factory: The Industrial Ideal in American Agriculture*, in which she notes, in relation to the farm crisis of the 1980s, "Those of us in cities could only wonder what had gone wrong. Why would farm families overextend themselves so dramatically? Why would they take out loans that they could not live long enough to repay? Why were they investing in expensive livestock confinement systems or sophisticated field machines when they were already in debt?"[40] Importing a nonrural value—that of maximized commodity production without regard for

38. Cramer, *The Politics of Resentment*, 59.

39. See Wuthnow, *The Left Behind*, 101–102, or Cramer, *The Politics of Resentment*, 61.

40. Fitzgerald, *Every Farm a Factory*, 1–2. For further analysis of this subject, see also Kathryn Marie Dudley, *Debt and Dispossession: Farm Loss in America's Heartland* (University of Chicago, 2000), particularly chaps. 1 and 2, or Peggy F. Barlett, *American Dreams, Rural Realities: Family Farms in Crisis* (University of North Carolina, 1993).

family and small community vitality—precipitated what appeared to be nonsensical rural risk from the perspectives of nonrural onlookers. And as Fitzgerald notes, even within agriculture, this story has similar echoes throughout American history.[41]

With regard to the contemporary dimensions of the rural-nonrural lifestyle divide, Cramer maintains that "although many rural residents resented cities, they did not necessarily want to live in one."[42] For the rural folks Cramer engaged, the ways of living associated with knowing everyone in a community, trusting one's neighbors, and being close to nature were seen as both significant lifestyle advantages and sources of pride.[43] There was a strong sense that these lifestyle values were incompatible with city living, and so decisions made from within city contexts regarding rural life are doomed to failure unless significant energy is spent—and from their perspectives, it rarely is—actually trying to understand the contours of rural and small-town existence. The first two aspects of rural consciousness, that urban centers of power neither listen to rural concerns nor afford them a fair share when distributive decisions are made, essentially ensure that this third aspect is likewise suspicious of nonrural life.

Wuthnow terms one governing value of this rural lifestyle "common sense," which he defines in a rural perspective as "behaving as other people do and thus being trustworthy."[44] Recall that the rural moral community is identified not simply by feeling at home but also by doing the right things. Those right things are distillations of local tradition and wisdom, meaning that when someone acts against what members of a moral community expect as common sense, that person puts a distance between them and the moral community in terms not simply of predictability but of trust. Extrapolated to a communal level, when a nonrural body (city, government agency, corporation, etc.) acts

41. Fitzgerald, *Every Farm a Factory*, 2.

42. Cramer, *The Politics of Resentment*, 67.

43. Cramer, *The Politics of Resentment*, 67.

44. Wuthnow, *The Left Behind*, 107.

in a way that is out of sync with a moral community's common sense, the implication is not simply that the action is nonsensical; there is also the concern that such nonsense will be imposed ham-fistedly on rural areas by those who neither understand nor care about them. In Wuthnow's view, this is especially apparent in rural distrust of government, particularly at the federal level.[45]

A final facet of the perceived lifestyle gap that conditions rural consciousness, though this has certainly not been an exhaustive list, is rural attitudes concerning the necessity of hard work. Cramer points out that rural residents from both sides of the political spectrum in her study carried a sense that to inhabit a rural space brought with it a special requirement for hard work.[46] This, of course, didn't mean that there was political consensus regarding how to interpret that social value—Republicans tended to claim "the demands of rural life simply required hard work," while Democrats suggested more that "living in a rural place meant that it was especially tough to make ends meet, even if you worked hard"[47]—but valuing hard work as integral to a rural lifestyle seemed to be a universal sense. As above, that this is a distinguishing characteristic does not make it unique to rural areas, but to place value on it as a lifestyle requirement is an important aspect of rural consciousness. Being able to do hard work is only part of the point, and actually doing the hard work is likewise only part of the point; *choosing* to live in a place and in a way that *requires* and *values* hard work gets closer to this sense of rural consciousness.

It is a fair question to ask whether the perspective of rural consciousness actually stands up to data-driven scrutiny. Cramer explores exactly this question in the fourth chapter of *Resentment*, and by compiling and interpreting data surrounding unemployment, household income, tax expenditures versus taxes paid, and a host of other factors, she concludes that "there are solid and understandable empirical reasons

45. Wuthnow, *The Left Behind*, 98–110.

46. Cramer, *The Politics of Resentment*, 72–73.

47. Cramer, *The Politics of Resentment*, 73.

that rural folks might think that they are the victims of distributive injustice."[48] To be clear, Cramer is simply making the case that rural consciousness is neither incoherent nor necessarily untenable. It is a distinguishable, contextually rooted set of perspectives that appears to emerge not as a result of indoctrination distributed by mass or local media but instead, in Cramer's words, "because we teach these things to each other."[49] Wuthnow's account of the moral community in this way finds some validation in Cramer's research; the moral community is a space of home, of obligation, of support, and of shared values, and part of the operation of that community is cultivating a shared sense of what it *means* to live rural life. It is about more than location or relatively low population density; rural life is about inhabiting a particular socially structured context (the rural moral community) infused with a particular contextual perspective (rural consciousness).

Shared Narratives Between Rural and Nonrural America

Not all commentators concur that rural America is actually a distinguishable entity or concept. For some, reckoning with the rural-nonrural divide is more about exposing false narratives about rural America that stubbornly persist in rural and nonrural imaginations alike. Understanding rural perspectives, in the view of Daniel Immerwahr, "will require setting myths aside and grappling with what the rich and the powerful have done to rural spaces and people."[50] Immwerwahr writes this in a review of historian Stephen Conn's book *The Lies of the Land*, in which Conn essentially concludes that energy spent trying to understand rural America as a distinct social, cultural, or economic

48. Cramer, *The Politics of Resentment*, 110.

49. Cramer, *The Politics of Resentment*, 110.

50. Daniel Immerwahr, "Beyond the Myth of Rural America," *New Yorker*, October 16, 2023, https://www.newyorker.com/magazine/2023/10/23/beyond-the-myth-of-rural-america.

context is at best wasted effort.[51] Instead, he claims, a more historically honest conception of rural America is essentially reducible to spaces of low population density. Attempting to understand rural areas of the United States as *places* in the sense of spaces that are saturated with cultural and social meaning[52] is a fool's errand: "Whatever sense of place the term *rural* once engendered, it has largely evaporated."[53] While I am unconvinced of Conn's central thesis for reasons that will become apparent later in the book, his historical analysis is illuminative for the way it shows clearly identifiable cultural, social, and economic resonances between rural and nonrural contexts in the United States. As such, Conn is the primary interlocutor for this section, which focuses on three narrative resonances he names: (1) militarization, (2) industrialization, and (3) big business and chain stores.

For Conn, one significant similarity between rural and nonrural contexts in the United States is the presence of systems defined and controlled by the American military. Military bases themselves have a tendency to become nonrural spaces eventually, and Conn assumes it is self-evident that the US military has had considerable impact on nonrural areas. Many, however, like Fort Hood, which Conn examines, began as rural.[54] In the case of Fort Hood, even its establishment was not an easy, amicable thing: Conn notes that "nearly 1,200 landowners in Coryell County alone had their property taken from them in order that the army and its tanks could roll in . . . On March 9, [1942], James Stevenson, about to lose his farm, spent the day sitting on his front porch insisting to his friends that he wasn't going to move. Then he killed himself—the first of several suicides among those who had their

51. Stephen Conn, *The Lies of the Land: Seeing Rural America for What It Is—and Isn't* (University of Chicago, 2023), 249, 252.

52. For an in-depth discussion of spaces and p(l)aces, see Anthony Pinn, *The End of God-Talk: An African-American Humanist Theology* (Oxford University, 2012), esp. chaps. 1–3.

53. Conn, *The Lies of the Land*, 255.

54. Conn, *The Lies of the Land*, esp. chap. 2.

homes confiscated."[55] The story of Fort Hood culminates for Conn in its current state of nonrurality, next to Killeen, "a strip-mall townscape of lowest-common-denominator retail catered to the tens of thousands of men, most of them under thirty, who cycled in and out of the base."[56] The rural metamorphosed into the nonrural through a process of dissolution, reorganization, and military-personnel-driven development.

Military bases are not the whole picture from Conn's perspective. The development of particular military bases is an episodic phenomenon, even if it participates in a larger narrative of rural militarization. What really holds together the narrative of rural militarization is Conn's description of the history of the US Army Corps of Engineers. In his words, "with the possible exception of the Homestead Act, no other federal enterprise has transformed the landscape of the nation, and rural spaces in particular, more than the US Army Corps of Engineers."[57] In the early history of the United States, the military conquest of native peoples made it relatively obvious that the nation's development was first a military operation. That set the stage for both rural and nonrural land and water to be subject to military assessment and modification, leading Conn to conclude that "given how extensively the corps has reengineered American watersheds, one is hard pressed to find too many rural spaces that haven't, in the end, been altered by the Army Corps of Engineers."[58]

Conn's point in laying out this history is to provide an accurate backdrop for the current widespread support for and entanglement with the US military that finds a ready home in many areas of rural America. Rural Americans tend to be overrepresented in the branches of the military. Conn notes that by 2007, "roughly half of the Americans killed in Iraq came from towns of under 25,000 people," and "nearly 40 percent of the veterans of the Iraq and Afghanistan wars who returned home

55. Conn, *The Lies of the Land*, 41.

56. Conn, *The Lies of the Land*, 51.

57. Conn, *The Lies of the Land*, 31.

58. Conn, *The Lies of the Land*, 33.

resided in rural areas,"[59] pointing to what Conn reads as a contradiction: "On the one hand, rural families have suffered loss and grief as a result of the 'war on terror' much more than the rest of us. At the same time, they want—they need—to support the military unflaggingly . . . because the military gives them their sense of American identity and their system of values, and in a very real way, their sense of family."[60] The voracity of Conn's conjecture in this notwithstanding, there remains an important point in this for the purposes of our discussion: Assuming that rural America cannot lay exclusive or distinctive claim to the US military, militarization is a narrative with significant resonance between rural and nonrural America.

This subjection of rural spaces to the centralized oversight of military authority set the stage for the operation of other large, nonrural authorities to exert significant influence on the development and redevelopment of rural spaces in the United States, particularly through industrialization. Conn notes that in the years between the Civil War and the turn of the twentieth century, industry in the United States had become largely localized in urban areas.[61] This gave rise to a strong political impulse to "decentralize" American industry throughout the twentieth century, both to slow the exodus of rural Americans to urban areas and to make use of what was perceived as the relatively easily accessible wide-open space of rural contexts for industrial development.

Accounts of industrialization in rural America have at times paid excessive attention specifically to the industrialization of agriculture. While Conn concurs that the roots of rural industrialization can be found in Theodore Roosevelt's Country Life Commission ("largely an urban phenomenon that projected its own fantasies about country life onto a rural canvas"),[62] the process gained significant steam under the leadership of Franklin Roosevelt, who "saw the New Deal as a way to

59. Conn, *The Lies of the Land*, 74.

60. Conn, *The Lies of the Land*, 75.

61. Conn, *The Lies of the Land*, 79–80.

62. Conn, *The Lies of the Land*, 88.

rescue and revive rural America."[63] During this period, "agrarian intellectuals" held significant influence in United States policymaking, and rural American infrastructure and industry gleaned significant benefits as a result.[64] However, as industrial decentralization unfolded relatively successfully up through the 1970s, it became less and less clear that nonindustrial endeavors (agricultural or not) could survive in rural areas any more than they could survive in nonrural ones.[65] This movement from agrarianism to wholesale industrialization was at least partially intentional; legislation like the 1972 Rural Development Act provided incentives and advantages for industrial interests to move into rural areas, and initiatives like this met with reasonable success. As Conn notes, "By the 1990s, 20 percent of all American factory jobs were located in the countryside."[66]

As industry flourished in rural spaces of the United States, the late twentieth century saw an increased emphasis not simply on industrialization but also on significant growth of corporations and businesses, both agricultural and not. Within agriculture, this largely amounted to a repudiation of the norms that had been established in and after the New Deal, supplanted by a conviction that farmers should "produce as much as possible, all the time."[67] This idea may seem unremarkable, but it represents a significant shift away from ideals like land stewardship and toward ideals of production by any means necessary, including land and environmental exploitation. This shift was enshrined in governmental policy through the actions of Earl Butz, US Secretary of

63. Conn, *The Lies of the Land*, 89.

64. For a detailed analysis of this phenomenon, see Jess Gilbert, *Planning Democracy: Agrarian Intellectuals and the Intended New Deal* (Yale University, 2016).

65. Deborah Fitzgerald's account of the agrarian adoption of the "industrial ideal" through the early parts of the twentieth century makes clear that whatever American agriculture was to become afterward, it would be significantly impacted by industrialization (see Fitzgerald, *Every Farm a Factory*, esp. chaps. 4 and 6).

66. Conn, *The Lies of the Land*, 111.

67. Conn, *The Lies of the Land*, 162.

Agriculture from 1971 to 1976, whom Conn largely blames for strong-arming American agriculture into corporate industrialization: "What was new was that the changes to federal policy over which Butz presided aligned federal goals with corporate ones, thus enabling agribusiness to cement its hold on American farm production and on farmers themselves."[68] Whatever nonindustrial ideals rural America may have harbored in contradistinction to nonrural America, the 1970s and afterward made it very difficult to distinguish between the values and operations of rural industry versus nonrural industry.

As agriculture and other sectors of rural American economic life became industrialized, they also became increasingly welcoming to large businesses, resonating with the development of large business in nonrural areas. Conn points out that the development of two powerhouse chain stores of the twentieth century—Woolworth's and J. C. Penney—flourished in small towns.[69] The explosive expansion of these chains maps quite neatly onto the years during which American agriculture flirted with and then largely adopted the industrial ideal described by Fitzgerald,[70] and while by 1949, the *number* of these and other chain stores had dropped significantly, Conn maintains that decline was mostly "store consolidations, not simply store closures. Fewer stores, but bigger ones."[71] These chain stores sought to provide goods to "up-and-coming" rural communities, who kept them afloat relatively well up until the 1970s and 1980s. By then, as rural agriculture and industry shifted from New Deal ideology and policy to that of Nixon and Butz, these chain stores began to die out. The corporatization of rural America, it seems, has squeezed much of the "up-and-coming" out of rural communities.

In Conn's view, an apt illustration of this fall of one kind of big business in rural America is the rise of another kind: that of stores like

68. Conn, *The Lies of the Land*, 167.

69. Conn, *The Lies of the Land*, 173–184.

70. Fitzgerald, *Every Farm a Factory*, 21–29.

71. Conn, *The Lies of the Land*, 185.

Dollar General and Walmart. In Conn's view, these companies essentially seek out the inverse of what their predecessors like Woolworth's and J. C. Penny did; whereas the earlier generation of chains made a home in rural America to capitalize on a burgeoning rural economy, Walmart and Dollar General appear to have business models predicated on rural poverty. Particularly in the case of Dollar General, Conn explains that "[the] eighteen thousand Dollar General locations map rural poverty to an exacting degree. If Woolworth sought out the up-and-coming in rural America, Dollar General searches for the down-and-out."[72]

Conn paints a damning picture of Dollar General and its owners, pointing out its history of labor violations, its wholesale apathy regarding the well-being of communities into which it inserts itself, its general disregard for safe levels of staffing and security, and its bad pay and insistence on overworking its employees.[73] The cruel irony that Conn clearly names is that in the context of these failings, the self-understanding of Dollar General's ownership nevertheless seems to be that their business embodies "small-town values" and does so in "explicitly Christian terms."[74] There seems to be precious little of the moral community or rural consciousness that finds healthy expression in the operations of Dollar General, and in that sense this represents another resonance between rural and nonrural spaces of the United States. Where poverty and hardship exist, there are often efficient enterprises that seek to exploit rather than alleviate that poverty and hardship. As Conn notes, "Dollar General relies on impoverished people, and it needs them to stay impoverished. 'Our low-income customer base is part of a growing market,' Dollar General's chief administrative officer said, tone deaf to the commentary he was making about rural America and about American society altogether."[75] At least in this case, Conn's depiction

72. Conn, *The Lies of the Land*, 191.

73. Conn, *The Lies of the Land*, 192–199.

74. Conn, *The Lies of the Land*, 194, 199.

75. Conn, *The Lies of the Land*, 200.

of the myth of rural and small-town America has largely been silent or impotent in responding to this kind of big business exploitation. In contemporary American rural spaces, as in nonrural ones, big business often has the final say.

Conclusion: Narrative, Myth, Tradition

In the picture of rural America I have painted in this chapter, I have regularly referred to what I see as the main aspects of its identity as "narratives." I do so knowing full well the likelihood that the central interlocutors of the chapter (Wuthnow, Cramer, and Conn) might not describe their understandings of rural America as narratives. My intention is not to co-opt their work and call it something it isn't. Rather, the fact that these representatives from three distinct academic disciplines—sociology, political science, and history, respectively—craft similarly distinct understandings of rural American reality (or its lack, in Conn's case) points exactly to my central concern for the chapter. That is, it is important to contextualize rural America not as reducible to a structure or a demographic or political persuasion but as a social reality with multiple overlapping and sometimes competing stories that nevertheless all point to truths of that reality. These stories about what rural America is or is not are important because they influence what rural America can or will become. That's what narrative does; it speaks a story that forms and reforms its subject matter, its tellers, and its hearers. In doing so, it interacts with other narratives that similarly exert formative influence on those who participate in them, and a pastiche of story takes shape that dances with truth without artificially reducing it to discursive definition.

Some might argue that what I'm describing here is myth rather than narrative, and I readily admit that there is some overlap between the two concepts. However, the problem with myth in contemporary American society is that it tends to be tied to accusations of falsehood, as is the case when Conn and those who resonate with him speak of the myth of rural America. The implication is that the myth obscures what is real rather than reveals it. In this view, if rural America is a myth, then we ought to demythologize it in order to precipitate out whatever crystals of truth it might be holding in suspension.

Part of the reason I am not drawn to the idea of rural America as a myth is that both myth and its demythologizing tend to value coherence as a criterion for voracity. In some cases, of course, this is necessary, but I have become less and less convinced that coherence is a helpful measure by which to evaluate the vitality or existence of a social context. Doing so often requires observers or interpreters to "resolve" mythological or demythologized incoherence according to the ideologies and proclivities of the interpreter. In the case of much of rural America, this is exactly the kind of problem that rural consciousness reacts against: the imposition of external, paternalistic simplifications of a complex rural reality in order to fit nonrural sensibilities of what "really" must be the case. Narrative, by contrast, rarely suffers such scruples of coherence. Narratives can be ambiguous, in tension with one another, and even in some cases contradictory or paradoxical, and they can still speak truth together (perhaps it bears repeating that my home academic discipline is theology). Rural America is not a myth, but its vitality is sustained at least in part by the formative narratives that define it.

The reception of narratives, their propagation, and activities of handing them on can also be called *tradition*. In my own research in rural Christian congregations, nearly every interviewee spoke at least once about the importance of tradition in their understanding of both religious and social life. Often, in their view, the task of handing on—which is the etymological root of the word *tradition*—and practicing tradition transcended any divide they would have named between the social and the religious. In the rural Christian congregations we studied, interviewees' sense of rural identity was built by stories—narratives—of belonging in a place, knowing everyone, sharing values, being subject to community obligation, and benefiting from community support (in short, all the aspects of Wuthnow's rural moral community), and their understanding of rural Christian identity derived from exactly these same narratives. These narratives were not always coherent, but they painted a picture of tradition in rural American Christianity that was beholden to the established, locally, communally accepted ways of doing things. As one interviewee explained when we asked about what they saw as the most meaningful or important things their church does, "We do a lot of community things. I think a lot of the traditional ways the church looks at life are trying to get modernized . . . and I have challenges with that because of my age and growing up in a certain way."[76] In the view of this rural Christian, history, community, upbringing, and religious practice all find voice in what they perceive as most meaningful in their rural church's life. The narratives of each of these facets of their existence did not need to align perfectly; in the experience of this interviewee and others we spoke with, to be rural and to be Christian both looked a lot like the narrative of the rural moral community.

I emphasize this resonance with the rural moral community narrative not because we didn't see reflections of the other narratives in our research but simply because this resonance was so consistently present. Rural consciousness, for its part, provides a helpful way to conceptualize common rural perspectives associated with distrust of external power structures that rural folks often feel do not take adequate account of rural needs or concerns, a sense that rural areas consequently experience some level of distributive injustice, and a vision of lifestyle and values that they often see as distinct from their nonrural counterparts. Conn's analysis, on the other hand, has provided a helpful corrective against drawing too stark a distinction between the rural and nonrural. The impacts of American militarization, industrialization, and big business have unfolded similarly in both rural and nonrural contexts of the United States, and that commonality is worthwhile to keep in mind so as not to conjecture that rural America is some sort of independent entity separate from the rest of American society.

All this said, part of the problem with struggling to uncover or construct a workable definition of the rural is that many who have attempted to do so have not taken adequate, or sometimes any, account of the role of symbol in constructing their conception of rural social

76. Anonymized interviewee, recorded interview with Lydia Mattern, summer 2022.

reality and contextual perspectives. Indeed, such a thing might not even strike some of them as particularly important to do. However, symbol plays an essential role in defining and redefining the contours of narrative, and a frustratingly common misstep when symbol garners any attention at all is to pass over it as essentially reducible to something like literary representation or a self-evident aspect of ritual practice. In order to address this challenge and move the discussion closer to a socially and theologically responsible treatment of symbol, the following chapter engages two necessary tools for crafting the foundation on which to build a tenable understanding of symbol in relation to social ethics: first, a theory of social structures, critical realist social theory, that is capable of taking sufficient account of rural social reality and, second, an approach to ritual studies that paves the way for understanding the social function of symbol in both its ritual and non-ritual functions.

CHAPTER TWO

Seeing the Rural Through Critical Realism and Ritual Studies

Introduction: The Place of Theory

HAVING SKETCHED IN chapter 1 a series of narratives evocative of rural American social reality, it is necessary to be clear about what is meant by *social reality* in the first place. In doing so, my goal is not to retreat from social narrative and practice into the vapor of theoretical abstraction. Theory and practice are mutually dependent for their vitality, accuracy, clarity, and precision. To neglect one is to allow the other to suffer, and while the overarching goal of this project, to facilitate engaging the symbolic depth of rural social reality responsibly when doing social ethics, is admittedly more practical than theoretical, that practical goal does not supplant the need to engage relevant theorizing. As Margaret Archer, one of the primary conversation partners of this chapter, notes, "Theory has to be useful and usable: it is not an end in itself . . . society has to be tackled *in* theory and *for* practice. These two tasks cannot be separated, for were practical utility to be the whole criterion we would commit ourselves to instrumentalism—to working with theoretically ungrounded rules of thumb."[1]

In engaging theory and returning to practice, this chapter centers on two strains of theorization that are illuminative for the interplay between symbol and social ethics in rural social contexts. First, the chapter focuses on theorizing the social, consulting critical realist

1. Margaret S. Archer, *Realist Social Theory: The Morphogenetic Approach* (Cambridge University, 1995), 135.

sociology (also called *critical realist social theory*).[2] While the critical realist understanding of social reality has been around at least since the 1990s—and its epistemological predecessor finds its root in philosophies of science from the 1970s[3]—its impact on theological ethics is far more recent and has been gaining steam.[4] A major reason for this is the robust way by which critical realist sociology can take account of both individual and collective agency—and the combination of the two—in social structures without reducing collective agency into individualism or individual agency into collectivism.[5] Theological ethicists and others[6] have also recognized the utility of how critical realist sociology envisions the stratified nature of human and natural existence, as well as its approach to the concept of emergence, or the idea that the "layers" of stratified reality are not reducible to one another, but rather are often unpredictable and increasing in complexity. These facets together constitute a vision of social reality that is ripe for conversation with rural American contexts where moral community and rural

2. These are not the only two terms by which this approach of theorization is known. It is also sometimes called *realist social theory* or simply *critical realism*. For this discussion, I will usually use the term *critical realist sociology* since that appears to be the most common way to refer to it in theological ethics, but on occasion, I will call it *critical realist social theory* when I intend to emphasize its theorizing role.

3. Many of which have seen reprintings since then. See Roy Bhaskar, *A Realist Theory of Science* (Routledge, 2008).

4. See, for example, the essays in Daniel K. Finn, ed., *Moral Agency Within Social Structures and Culture: A Primer on Critical Realism for Christian Ethics* (Georgetown University, 2020).

5. The relationships between structure and agency are also captured well from a critical realist perspective in Christian Smith, *What Is a Person?: Rethinking Humanity, Social Life, and the Moral Good from the Person Up* (University of Chicago, 2010).

6. See, for example, Finn, "What Is a Sinful Social Structure?," as well as David Cloutier, "Sociological Self-Knowledge, Critical Realism, and Christian Ethics," *Studies in Christian Ethics* 34, no. 2 (2021): 158–170; Benjamin Durheim, "Epicletic Advance? Viewing Eucharistic Fellowship Through Critical Realism and the Epiclesis," *Proceedings of the North American Academy of Liturgy* (2020): 87–101; or Benjamin Durheim, "Converting Consumerism: A Liturgical-Ethical Application of Critical Realism," *Religions* 10, no. 5 (May 2019): 1–13.

consciousness may appear operatively distinct from nonrural contexts, even while rural America shares significant history and social narratives with nonrural America.

Having laid a social-theoretical foundation, the chapter then takes a step toward symbol and symbolization. To do so, the chapter engages the field of ritual studies, especially as it appears in the work of Catherine Bell. Bell's scholarship has been influential in Christian liturgical and sacramental theology for a while now,[7] and she is an ideal interlocutor with whom to set the stage for a sustained analysis of how symbol functions social-ethically. One reason for this is that symbols and rituals enjoy a kind of popular association with each other; when one thinks of symbols, one tends to think of rituals and vice versa. This became clear in my 2023 research in a rural Christian liturgical community, which was focused on the interplay between the symbols that church community used and the social outlooks of its members. In our conversations, interviewees needed no prompting at all to connect symbol to ritual. When we asked about symbols, they would almost always begin by speaking about their experiences of church services, initiation rites, or other ritualized embodiments of Christian piety. It was often less apparent to them, however, that symbols may also function socially, outside of rituals themselves. Since one of the aims of this project is to make the case that there is a depth of symbolic reality that helps ground social existence (*not* limited to ritual or religion), beginning with a social space where that is already relatively obvious—ritual—makes sense.

Bell's work is also helpful for the way she structures her own ritual theory. She intentionally departs from treating ritual as a kind of special, isolated, set-aside activity that is socially unique and instead treats ritual as an endemic part of the larger milieu of human

---

7. See, for example, Kimberly Hope Belcher, *Efficacious Engagement: Sacramental Participation in the Trinitarian Mystery* (Liturgical Press, 2011), esp. chaps. 2 and 4; Joseph Favazza, "The Efficacy of Ritual Resistance: The Case of Catholic Sacramental Reconciliation," *Worship* 72, no. 3 (1998): 210–220; or John D. Laurance, "Catherine Bell and Liturgical Theology," *Antiphon* 4, no. 2 (1999): 14–18.

social practices. In her words, ritual activities should be "restored to the context of social activity in general . . . I propose a focus on 'ritualization' as a strategic *way* of acting and then turn to explore how and why this way of acting differentiates itself from other practices."[8] If ritual activity shares its social substance with the rest of social reality as opposed to being somehow isolated from it, then it becomes a logical step to conclude that ritual symbols also participate in the same social substance as the rest of social reality. Additionally, while Bell's work is inclusive of religious rituals in particular, her scholarly attention spans a far wider array of rituals (including nonreligious festivals, political rituals, etc.), allowing her to substantiate ritualization as a social phenomenon that is not necessarily reducible to religion or sect.[9] This also is helpful for our purposes, as it invites the question of how symbolization can or does—or does not—achieve intelligibility and, ultimately, legibility.

Having laid a foundation and set a stage, the chapter concludes by returning from theory to practice. The final section of the chapter relates several narrative examples drawn from rural experience and reads them through the lenses of critical realist sociology and Bell's approach to ritual theory. The goal in this is not to abstract from the narratives what might be conjectured to be *really* going on—that would be to make the same mistake we warned against in chapter 1. Instead, these narratives serve as something like test cases for our theoretical foundation laying and stage setting, making space for a discernment of whether the theorization is sufficiently accurate and relevant (I argue that it is). The final section also serves to refocus the project on its longer trajectory: to move into a theologically sufficient understanding of symbol and symbolization capable of making sense of rural societal ritual and reality.

---

8. Catherine Bell, *Ritual Theory, Ritual Practice* (Oxford University, 1992), 7. Emphasis in original.

9. See Bell, *Ritual: Perspectives and Dimensions*, esp. chap. 4.

Critical Realist Sociology

The seminal work of critical realist sociology is Margaret Archer's text *Realist Social Theory: The Morphogenetic Approach*, and in terms of its relevance for theological ethics, it has been the work of Daniel Finn that has led the way in bringing critical realist sociology to bear.[10] Drawing from the realist theory of science described and advocated by Roy Bhaskar,[11] Archer adapts that theoretical framework to the purposes and goals of sociology. Frustrated by what she saw as the inadequacies of both sides of the individualist versus collectivist debate regarding how agency and freedom function socially, Archer argues that any acceptable social theorizing must be able to take sufficient account of the extent to which—and mechanisms by which—individual and collective agency interact.[12] In order to do so, Archer largely refrains from adjudicating between the two opposing perspectives and instead grounds her argument about agency not *in* agency itself but in the makeup of human society. Her theory, as well as some of how it has been used in theological ethics and elsewhere, can be broken down into (1) the stratified nature of reality and the concept of emergence, (2) Archer's "morphogenetic approach" to social change and development, and (3) the implications of critical realist sociology for understanding how agency and social change interact.

Emergence is a term that refers to the process by which lower-order realities may combine or interact to form higher-order realities. Lower-order and higher-order in this case do not connote *better* and *worse* or even *more desirable* and *less desirable*. They mean the degree to which

10. Archer, *Realist Social Theory*. It was Daniel Finn who first introduced me to critical realism, and his work has been essential for my own thinking about how social reality functions. See especially Daniel Finn's landmark article "What Is a Sinful Social Structure?"

11. See Bhaskar, *A Realist Theory of Science*, as well as Stanley E. Porter and Andrew W. Pitts, "Critical Realism in Context," *Journal for the Study of the Historical Jesus* 13 (2015): 276–306, along with the essays in Margaret Archer et al., eds., *Critical Realism: Essential Readings* (Routledge, 1998).

12. Archer, *Realist Social Theory*, 33–34.

realities have made something together. As Daniel Finn explains, "The simplest example of emergence is water, which exists at a 'higher' level than do the oxygen and hydrogen atoms that combined to produce it. Water emerges from this combination of elements and is entirely dependent on them for its existence, yet it possesses characteristics that neither hydrogen nor oxygen does."[13] It is important to note in this example that emergence does not necessarily indicate a "progression" of sorts, moving toward some end goal or completion. Water is not a "more complete" form of hydrogen and oxygen, as both hydrogen and oxygen have their own respective properties and being that are not necessarily ordered toward the *telos* of becoming water. Likewise, emergence is not a kind of platonic measure of "how real" a thing might be. Emergence describes difference and complexity, doing so by including an ontological genealogy of dependence and components (i.e., it describes the constitutive building blocks of a thing that make it a thing). It connotes where a thing comes from and indicates that the emergent thing is not reducible to its component parts.

Emergence, as one might expect, is also not limited to just one or a few progressions. If water and salt (both emergent entities) are combined with flour and yeast (both results of a great many emergences, from their elemental foundations on up), then under the right circumstances and care, bread will emerge. The bread is not reducible to its four ingredients, and it has properties—and uses—that differ from the things that made it up. All of reality is made up of these layers of emergence, which calls for some kind of organizational principle to make sense of them. This principle is the stratification of reality, which emphasizes the distinctions between higher-level and lower-level entities and phenomena. One should not expect hydrogen and oxygen to behave as water does, nor expect water, salt, yeast, or flour to behave as bread does. However, while that might seem obvious, there has been a strong tendency in the Western intellectual tradition to strive to reduce entities

13. Daniel K. Finn, ed., "What Is Critical Realism?," in *Moral Agency Within Social Structures and Culture: A Primer on Critical Realism for Christian Ethics* (Georgetown University, 2020), 20.

and phenomena to their observable and component parts and thereby deny the reality of anything beyond those parts. This is classic Western empiricism,[14] which is one of the targets of Roy Bhaskar's critiques when he crafted his realist approach to science.[15] The main problem with empiricism, Bhaskar thought, and Archer builds on this, is that if one reduces what is real to what can be perceived by the senses, one misses real emergent relations between the entities of reality. Emergence, in a sense, shifts focus away from objects and toward how those objects relate or interact.

Finn uses the example of a book falling to the floor to illustrate this attention to relations: "Newton's 'law' of gravity is a human statement that points to real forces in the universe . . . it is the relation between the book and the earth that causes it to fall. Gravity is not a law but instead a force. It is an emergent property of the relation between the book and the earth."[16] In this way, critical realism can differentiate among three "domains" of reality, as opposed to empiricism's single domain of sense perceptibility. First, the domain of the empirical includes everything that is perceived (to that degree, at least, critical realism makes use of empiricism); second, the domain of the actual includes all that takes place but may or may not be perceived; third, the domain of the real is made up of all that exists, including forces and relations that govern the empirical and the actual.[17] In a word, critical realism understands the world in terms of what is observed (the empirical), what happens (the actual), and what *is* (the real).

For Archer, Finn, and other proponents of critical realist sociology, this view of reality as stratified and entities as emergent allows for an

---

14. Even in his introductory article for critical realism, Daniel K. Finn indicts David Hume, John Stuart Mill, and others as crafting this perspective and enshrining it as a litmus test for responsible scientific inquiry (Finn, "What Is Critical Realism?," 21–22).

15. See Bhaskar, *A Realist Theory of Science*, esp. 12–20.

16. Finn, "What Is Critical Realism?," 23.

17. Finn, "What Is Critical Realism?," 24.

understanding of society that does not reduce what is "real" to only that which is sense perceptible. Instead, the relations themselves between persons and communities are real and emergent, not reducible to only the persons and communities who participate in them. This insight makes possible, in Archer's view, a navigation of what she calls "the vexatious fact of society," by which she means the problem of understanding the relationship between social structures and the agencies (exercises of freedom) of the entities that make them up, without falling into either individualism or collectivism.[18] For Archer, social reality is made up of perceivable artifacts and persons but also of the myriad relations that govern how those persons and things interact. These relationships are not simply conjecture or perception or manipulations of reality; they are part of the *real* that society is.

A word may be warranted regarding what critical realist sociology means by a social "structure," as something distinct from "culture." In Finn's words, "The core of a social structure is the system of relations among the various social positions that make it up."[19] For example, a sports association emerges as a social structure by virtue of organizing relations of players, coaches, fans, staff, and/or other roles, but it is not reducible to the particular players, coaches, and so on that comprise it. Likewise, a business emerges as a social structure with particular roles assigned to leadership, management, employment, labor, and others. The relations among the offices of the business craft a structure—a real social thing—that particular members of the business live into. Culture, on the other hand, is less about relations among social positions than it is made up by "the entire 'world of ideas' available to a social group at a given time."[20] Culture is the contextual

---

18. Archer, *Realist Social Theory*, 1–16. See also Margaret S. Archer, *Being Human: The Problem of Agency* (Cambridge University, 2000).

19. Daniel K. Finn, ed., "Social Structures," in *Moral Agency Within Social Structures and Culture: A Primer on Critical Realism for Christian Ethics*(Georgetown University, 2020), 30.

20. Matthew A. Schadle, "Culture," in *Moral Agency Within Social Structures and Culture: A Primer on Critical Realism for Christian Ethics*, ed. Daniel K. Finn (Georgetown University, 2020), 47.

makeup that renders understanding possible within social life; as Archer describes it, "Culture as a whole is taken to refer to all intelligibilia, that is to any item which has the dispositional capacity of being understood by someone."[21] Culture is the intellectual and imaginational milieu of a society; structure connotes the relations that organize and govern how individual and communal entities live out their lives in that milieu.

Distinguishing in this way between structure and culture (something that is not unique to critical realists) allows Archer and other proponents of critical realist sociology to model how social change takes place without reducing the mechanisms of social change to cultural artifacts. This modeling is Archer's "morphogenetic approach," which is her way of describing how social change takes place with regard to structures. The basic model works in a repeating three-step process. First, in structural conditioning, the persons and communities of a society inherit and are formed by normative—and normalized—social relations (structures). These structures define a person's or group's role in that society, which can be as multifaceted as the society itself is. A person may be a laborer, a spouse, a minister, a parent, or any combination of these and myriad others. The structural weight of these roles lays out the cartography of the social actions that are available (or not) to the particular persons or groups within those roles. This is rarely a perfect process, in that one's understanding of one's roles is often limited, but the recognition of a role's existence *at all* bespeaks the operation of social-structural conditioning.

For example, if a person walks into a room and sees rows of chairs facing what appears to be the front of the room, and there is a person in the front speaking and writing on a board that is viewable to everyone else in the room while other persons are seated in the rows of chairs facing the single speaker, it is not necessary for that person to know exactly what a classroom is in order to have the weight of that particular classroom structure impressed upon them. The relations of the social structure have been defined prior to the visitor's coming and have laid real groundwork for the sociocultural interaction that takes place next.

---

21. Archer, *Realist Social Theory*, 180.

In the second step of the morphogenetic cycle, agents (whether individuals or groups) engage with each other and the structures by which their relations are defined. This is social interaction, though Archer calls it *sociocultural interaction* in an effort to acknowledge that structure and culture are easier to distinguish in theory than in practice.[22] In it, the agents' actions are subject to many overlapping layers of social costs and benefits that are both structurally and culturally defined. In the example of the classroom visitor, the visitor is free to take an open seat and listen to the teacher along with the rest of the class, or the visitor could walk to the front of the room and take over the teaching role, or the visitor could interrupt the class by loudly objecting to what the teacher is doing. Each of these options (and any number of others) carries implications for how the visitor is received and what kinds of interactions will be more or less easily available to that visitor in the future. Such implications take on flesh in the third step of the cycle.

The third step of the morphogenetic cycle is structural elaboration, in which the roles and relations (structures) of the social context are reformed in light of the social interactions that took place. For example, if the classroom visitor quietly took a seat and began taking notes, the class structure continues, having added another learner to the classroom. If the visitor proceeds to the front of the room and takes over teaching, the structure again stays largely the same, just with a different person in the teaching role. If the visitor interrupts the class with an objection or protest, the social structure now likely shifts because the structure had previously been one in which there was a teacher and learners, and now there is a new role that needs to be accommodated structurally: the visiting protestor. That interruption of the structural operation of the classroom does far more than simply introduce the content of the visitor's protest. It also forces a renegotiation of what the classroom is and what can acceptably take place within it. It is now a place that has included visiting protestors, which opens the second structural conditioning phase and sets the stage for the next social interaction step, and the cycle continues as visualized in figure 1.

22. Archer, *Realist Social Theory*, 156–158.

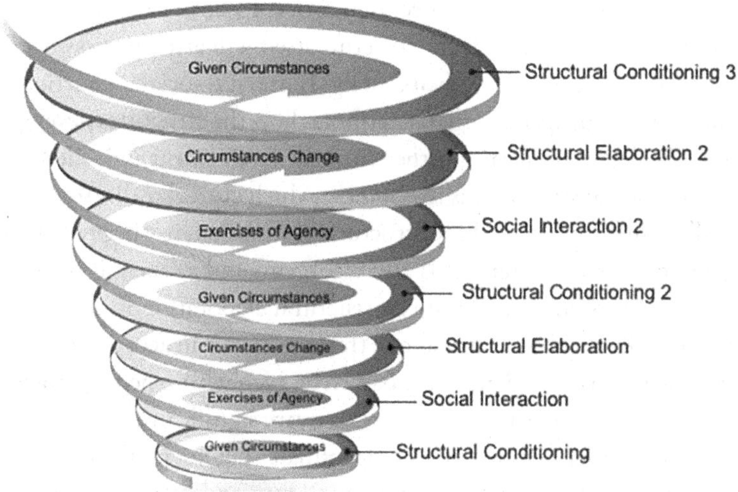

Figure 1.1. The morphogenetic cycle of structural change.[23]

One should note that while structures may change slightly or significantly as a result of social interactions, they may also simply be reinforced. Morphogenesis (social change) can also unfold as morphostasis (social reinforcement). In fact, social reinforcement may be the more common of the two, as it takes very little active exercise of agency in order to function. If all agents in a social context choose to live into their social relations as defined by the current structural system, that system renews its vitality. Whether this is a good thing or a bad thing depends on the particular social-structural context and the exercises of agency that take place. For example, living into and thereby affirming structures that incentivize or embody unjust relations between persons is complacency, but living into and affirming structures that are ordered toward

23. This figure comes from an earlier article I wrote engaging critical realist sociology (Durheim, "Epicletic Advance?"), and while it portrays the morphogenetic cycle in a visual that is distinct from the one Margaret Archer uses (see Archer, *Realist Social Theory*, 157, fig. 6), I think this more clearly shows the continuous emergent cycles of structural elaboration and/or reinforcement.

justice can unfold as resistance to injustice. In both cases, influences from within and without the structure itself will attempt to sway the structural system ("tilt the helix" of fig. 1), and it is social interaction—the interplay of agents—that determines how the structures develop.

This last point regarding the continual development and redevelopment of social structures is the point at which critical realist sociology really shines for social ethics. Structural elaboration may be predictable only to a certain extent; it is also emergent, and as such, it includes an element of unpredictability. Structural elaboration is, in a sense, indeterminate growth: Just as oak trees emerge from acorns, and their genetic material as identifiably oak trees, even while their number of branches or trunk shape or canopy size vary significantly, so also may the effects of social interactions be identifiable but not perfectly predictable. This is a feature of the system, not a bug, and it allows for a more comprehensible theorizing of social ethics than approaches that draw more deterministic cause-effect relationships between agents and social structures. From the perspective of critical realist sociology, emergence is the appropriate paradigm by which to understand social change or reinforcement, and that emergence is irreducibly conditioned by both individual and collective agency.

As an example, consider the visiting classroom protestor again. Entering the classroom and protesting is an exercise of individual agency (though possibly also collective agency if the protestor was sent there by a group), and the responses of the class and the teacher also unfold as both individual and collective agency. Perhaps the teacher responds by calling security and asking them to remove the protestor. The initial result is that the protestor may be removed from the classroom, but it is *not* certain what the continued structural elaboration will be. Perhaps this will be received by the student body or a particular related community as censorship or unjust silencing of a legitimate and needful voice. If so, the classroom structure now *also* includes recent history of, and sanction for, removal of protesting voices, and that may emanate beyond the particular classroom to the structure of the school itself and/or the communities that support it. On the other hand, removing the protestor may be received by the student body or related communities as a just protection of the structure needed for a particular learning environment. If that is the case, the structure now includes recent history of, and sanction for, that kind of protection, and likewise that will emanate beyond the classroom structure to the surrounding structures.

In both cases, however, if the goal of the teacher was to remove the protestor in order to *return* to the classroom as it was, that goal will have failed. Such a return is not possible. The morphogenetic cycle is more helical than it is cyclical, in that structures necessarily develop and/or strengthen as time moves forward. *How* they do so depends on a great many factors, including the particular social interactions that are baked into the cycle, as well as the diverse perspectives and understandings of which the structural conditioning consists. The formation of those perspectives is a function both of structure and of cultural components and operates on both an individual and communal level. This in turn pulls the discussion toward one authoritative mechanism by which those perspectives (and consequently their emergent relations and structures) are formed and reformed: ritual.

Theorizing Ritual

There is a wide expanse of space between having a general impression of something and having a specific understanding of what that thing is and how it functions. Ritual is a perfect example of this. Nearly everyone may have an impression of what a ritual is or how to recognize one when it is taking place, but it is a more difficult endeavor to coax out a discrete definition of ritual or ritualization. Folks may speak of ritual as reducible to routine (like the "morning ritual" one uses to begin the day), or as essentially a traditional practice (anything a community hands on through generations), or as something evocative of the spiritual, religious, or occult. Such a diversity of popular meanings invites scholarly attention and, for the purposes of our discussion, attention that clarifies the role and function of symbols in ritual. In such work of understanding ritual, few bodies of scholarship have been as influential as that of Catherine Bell.

Responding to an expansive array of writers on the concept of ritual,[24] Bell constructs a theory of ritual that centers not on the definition of ritual as a noun but on the process of what she calls "ritualization."[25] Ritualization, according to Bell, is "a way of acting that is designed and orchestrated to distinguish and privilege what is being done in comparison to other, usually more quotidian, activities."[26] Bell's methodological point in this is to approach ritual as a practice, a technical term whose content she draws principally from thinkers like Bourdieu,[27] meaning that in her view, ritualization unfolds as a social practice characterized by (at least) four distinctive features: It is "(1) situational; (2) strategic; (3) embedded in a misrecognition of what it is in fact doing; and (4) able to reproduce or reconfigure a vision of the order of power in the world."[28] Not all actions that share these features are therefore rituals, but ritualization functions in all four of these ways.

First, that ritualization is situational means that "much of what is important to it cannot be grasped outside of the specific context in which it occurs."[29] When a social action ritualizes, it may appear nonsensical, shallow, or unintelligible to outside observers. The content of ritualization is deeply contextual; it carries layers of meaning and implication that resist extraction or extrapolation to universality. This does not mean that ritualization is necessarily parochial or provincial, though ritualization, like any human practice, may exhibit those characteristics

---

24. Bell's work is suffused with engagement of other ritual theorists and those who have inspired them. See especially the first three chapters of Bell, *Ritual Theory, Ritual Practice*, and the first chapter of Bell, *Ritual: Perspectives and Dimensions*.

25. Bell, *Ritual Theory, Ritual Practice*, 140–142.

26. Bell, *Ritual Theory, Ritual Practice*, 74.

27. See Pierre Bourdieu, *Outline of a Theory of Practice* (Cambridge University, 1977).

28. Bell, *Ritual Theory, Ritual Practice*, 81.

29. Bell, *Ritual Theory, Ritual Practice*, 81.

as well. Instead, the situationality of ritualization means that it is born with a sustained connection to the concrete social body that forms it. Ritualization is a from-the-ground-up process, not a from-the-top-down process.

Second, ritualization as strategic means it is tied more to practical effectiveness than it is to intellectual or logical coherence. Bell notes that the "strategies" that unfold in ritualization are not necessarily intentional;[30] instead, they are operative, even organic tactical moves that emerge in the process of ritualization and serve to move the process along effectively. If ritualization can be thought of as the coming-to-be of a ritual, then the fact that it unfolds as strategic simply means that the actions that coalesce as ritualization exhibit a strategic, practical logic.

Third, thinking of ritualization in terms of a practice means that there is a misrecognition or misapprehension that surrounds the process itself, which is nevertheless necessary for the process to be successful. Bell gestures to the work of Jacques Derrida[31] (as well as that of Bourdieu) on the practice of gift-giving as an illustrative example of how this misrecognition works.[32] If one person gives another a gift, and particularly if the object that is exchanged has no intrinsic or monetary value, then an observer of the exchange might—correctly, in a sense—surmise either that nothing of value was exchanged or that the exchange could be interpreted in terms of credit and debit: One person gives something, which then incurs a debt for the other person, whether simply of gratitude or of a return gift or reciprocation of some

30. In this, her use of Bourdieu differs from Michel de Certeau's understanding of practice that distinguishes between strategies and tactics. See Michel de Certeau, *The Practice of Everyday Life* (University of California, 1988). Bell does acknowledge that Certeau makes this distinction between strategies and tactics but appears unperturbed by the distinction, as she is more concerned with explaining practice in relation to ritualization than practice as a concept itself.

31. Jacques Derrida, *Given Time: I. Counterfeit Money*, trans. Peggy Kamuf (University of Chicago, 1994) is especially illuminative in this, as is Jacques Derrida, *The Gift of Death*, trans. David Wills (University of Chicago, 1996).

32. Bell, *Ritual Theory, Ritual Practice*, 82.

kind. However, this obligation to return gratitude or reciprocation is "misrecognized" in the practice of gift-giving. If a person gives a gift *only in order to* receive a return gift or only in order to receive gratitude and renown, then that gift is compromised, in a sense, and becomes less of a gift. A gift exchange becomes more truly what it is (gratuitous and free) by this misrecognition of what is taking place. There is a kind of obligation that emerges in gift-giving, but it is obligation as seen through a glass darkly. It is a different kind of obligation than that of, say, market exchange, where obligation is quantified in terms of monetary value, but it is still some kind of obligation; it is misrecognized. Misrecognition in this case is essentially "seeing something differently." In a gift exchange, something of value has changed hands, but that exchange is kept deliberately separate from market-style obligation; it is *seen* as something else, something free and gratuitous. Likewise in ritualization, particular acts—washing, eating, gesturing, and so on—are misrecognized, not by becoming something else but by carrying meaning that is distinct from everyday washing, eating, gesturing, and so on. When an action undergoes ritualization, it remains the action, but it becomes an action misrecognized, an action that is both the same as it was and quite different.

The fourth characteristic of ritualization as a practice—that it forms and reforms how power takes on structure in a social context—Bell calls "redemptive hegemony,"[33] by which she means essentially "the symbolic framework that reigns as common-sense."[34] In a word, ritualization helps form what people take as obviously reasonable to do, think, or say. Common sense, for example, is a power that holds sway in a community, as we saw in chapter 1, but it neither exists in a vacuum nor develops without cause. Practices form the contours of a community's perspective of common sense, and ritualization plays a significant role in that formation process. That said, it would be a mistake to conclude that ritualization is therefore an efficient tool with which to produce

33. Bell, *Ritual Theory, Ritual Practice*, 83–86.

34. David Laitin, qtd. in Catherine Bell, *Ritual Theory, Ritual Practice*, 83.

an intended and desired synthetic common sense. As Bell argues, even though practices like ritualization do form and reform social power, the practice itself is not governed by an agent's intentional logic that envisions an ideal form of common sense: "A practice does not see itself do what it actually does."[35] Instead, when a practice like ritualization forms redemptive hegemony (or common sense), it does so in an unpredictable, emergent way. The ways that common sense orders power within a community are the results of all kinds of practices, but rarely, if ever, is that ordering reducible to a simple, efficient cause.

An example may paint this more clearly. In 2021, a group of students at the partnered institutions where I teach undertook a course of action that significantly harmed both the community's shared life and the lives of particular students in the community. The group—a number of male students living in a specific male-only dorm—had organized a "sex competition" in which they tried to see who could sleep with the most women students.[36] There was a justly significant outcry from the student body and others (faculty, alumni/ae, etc.), and in response, the College of Saint Benedict's Institute for Women's Leadership (IWL) organized a demonstration with the goals of demanding action from the school's administration and crafting a space for communal rebuke of the offending actions. None of this might easily be thought of as ritual, but the way the demonstration developed, took place, and worked its way into communal memory bespeaks a process of ritualization that maps well onto Bell's understanding of ritualization as a practice.

First, while the idea that there *was* a demonstration would be intelligible to a wide audience, its formation and impact are most legible from the standpoint of its embedded situation. The College of Saint

35. Bell, *Ritual Theory, Ritual Practice*, 87.

36. See Becca Most, "CSB/SJU Community Demands Action After Allegations of 'Sex Competition' Among Saint John's Students," *Saint Cloud Times*, October 21, 2021, https://www.sctimes.com/story/news/2021/10/21/students-demand-action-after-alleged-sex-competition-among-sju-students/8527264002/, or Associated Press, "CSB, SJU Investigate Alleged Sex Competition," *KNSI News*, October 20, 2021, https://knsiradio.com/2021/10/20/csb-sju-investigate-alleged-sex-competition/.

Benedict (historically a women's school) partners with Saint John's University (historically a men's school) in curriculum, classes, faculty, and key parts of administration. It was Saint John's students who perpetrated the "competition," and so the IWL discerned it would be best to hold the demonstration physically on the Saint John's campus, outdoors at a nexus point between several academic buildings, residence halls, and the dining hall. That center of foot traffic for the school's life became the location not of demonstrating generally but of demonstrating a particular set of things (in this case, the community's concern, indignation, and outrage in response to the actions of some of its members).

Second, while the demonstration's goals were relatively clear, the operative strategies in realizing those goals through the demonstration emerged through both its planning and the event itself. Both men and women students were invited to speak, and that and similar strategic moves prevented the event from being received as simply a rebuke aimed from one campus at the other; instead, it was largely received as the voice of the whole student body, a reception enhanced by the large number of students, faculty, staff, and community members who attended and participated. As the event unfolded, the third characteristic of ritualization as a practice emerged: Many attendees thought they were going to an event put on by a particular interest group on campus, and from a certain perspective that may have been the case. However, reducing the event to that interpretation is a misrecognition of what actually took place. I was teaching some sections of the school's introductory theology class that semester, and since we were moving through a module related to social ethics at the time, I asked students to attend the demonstration as either participants or observers, according to their preferences and convictions, and to reflect on their experience of the event. Nearly every reflection included some version of the same misrecognition and clarification (paraphrased here): "I didn't realize how many people in our community cared about something like this. This wasn't a demonstration by an isolated group; it was everyone." The demonstration moved from a discrete action to a ritualized practice as it morphed in its reception from an act by a *part* of the community to reconstituting in a different way what the community itself *was* in the minds of the students and participants.

Finally, this misrecognition spilled over into understandings of power, common sense, and what is "obvious" in this particular community. Part of this was on the side of administrative structure and action—the steps demanded by the IWL were nearly all implemented by the relevant power structures of the institutions—but that was not the whole of the demonstration's impact. Prior to the demonstration, in each of my classes, we discussed the "competition," and I asked students to consider together whether something like this was surprising or unexpected in the community, how that perception translates (or not) into its tacit acceptability or unacceptability, and why or why not that may be. The general consensus across the classes was that something like the competition was of course unacceptable but unsurprising. After the demonstration, however, we revisited those discussions in class, and there appeared a marked communal turn *toward* surprise. If so much of the community considered something like the competition unthinkable, how in the world did it become actual? Observation of and participation in the demonstration had played a part in shifting what was "common sense," away from a kind of implicit communal cynicism ("this is awful, but it's expected that groups will be awful sometimes") to something more akin to righteous indignation ("this is awful, and how could anyone think the community wouldn't respond as such?"). I have revisited this case study in every introductory theology class since, and while the consensus has not magically transformed as a whole, it has nevertheless never fully returned to that initial finding of the competition to be unacceptable yet unsurprising. The implications of this ritualized practice shifted something significant in the community's perception.

All this said, Bell does not simply collapse ritualization into practice itself. Ritualization is distinct from other practices by virtue of the fact that the community who ritualizes draws a particular distinction between what becomes ritualized and what does not. This may initially appear as tautologous (i.e., something is only ritualized if it is ritualized), but there is a truth hiding in that tautology. Whether a practice is ritualized or not depends on the separation that the community affords between that practice and other practices like it. In Bell's words, "Ritualization involves the very drawing . . . of a privileged distinction between ways of acting, specifically between those acts being performed and those being contrasted, mimed, or implicated."[37] In the case of the demonstration, it was a particular group crafting a space for particular voices to speak particular things. That was the practice. However, such a practice was separated from what actually happened by the sanction and reception of a much wider portion of the community. I doubt many, if any, of the participants would have called it a ritual, but the practice was ritualized by being perceived and received by the community as something *more* or *other* than just particular voices speaking within the community.

For Bell, this is the essence of what distinguishes ritualization from other practices a community undertakes. As she explains, "Ritualization, the production of ritualized acts, can be described, in part, as that way of acting that sets itself off from other ways of acting by virtue of the way in which it does what it does."[38] *What* a ritual does is not what makes it a ritual; it is *how* a ritual takes place that determines its ritualization. Such emphasis on the manner by which a practice unfolds opens the door to the importance of symbol. A ritual is not reducible to externally discernible actions; a ritual includes (and is constituted by) the *meanings* that are mediated by its practice. Eating and drinking are everyday practices, and taken from an external perspective or isolated as discrete actions, they mediate meaning that is not necessarily any deeper than bodily sustenance. However, if a community undertakes a particular *way* of eating and drinking—for example, eating bread and drinking wine after particular prayers and invocations of the divine have been proclaimed over them by a person who has been ritually assigned to that purpose—that eating and drinking become ritualized (as in the case of the Christian practice of Eucharist). Symbols proliferate and overlap in this practice, inclusive of the gathered community, the prayers being used, the timing, architecture,

37. Bell, *Ritual Theory, Ritual Practice*, 90.

38. Bell, *Ritual Theory, Ritual Practice*, 140.

environment, and many other aspects of the practice. Taken together, the practice mediates a meaning—participates in symbolization—far richer than the practice of simply eating and drinking. The ritualized practice connotes a symbolic depth that evokes power structures, aesthetics, senses of justice and truth, and all manner of community-embodied realities. Ritualization is the practice of a community speaking what is left unsaid.

Ritual, Critical Realist Sociology, and Symbol

It may be relatively obvious at this point how critical realist sociology and Bell's ritual theory are mutually evocative and supportive, but it may be helpful to name a few specific ways this is so. From the perspective of critical realist sociology, the collision of exercises of agency that precipitates ritualization depends on the social structures in which those agents are embedded (structural conditioning). Since structures, understood as real social relations that impact power and social landscape, provide something of the "beginning state" of a social practice,[39] working to understand the overlapping structures of a social context does more than simply increase one's awareness of a context's social development. Doing so also facilitates a "reading" of the misrecognitions, strategies, and other facets of social practices like ritualization. Additionally, this takes on particular significance when one reads what is happening in particular social interaction—there is more content in social interaction than simply the exercise of individual and collective agency. To the degree that social interactions are also social practices, particularly if they emerge as ritualization, they carry significant *non*-agential content that is nevertheless also real (i.e., Bell's insistence on ritualization's non-intentional strategies and non-agential reforming of power relations and common sense).

Reciprocally, while Bell's work does not dwell significantly on the concept of emergence, her understanding of ritualization resonates strongly with the conception of emergence held by critical realist

39. Though, strictly speaking, of course there is no clean "beginning state"; all of the morphogenetic cycle takes place *in media res*, with no recourse to anything like a clean social slate from which to begin.

sociology: that social realities can be and become real without being reducible to the individual parts that make them up and without deterministic predictability. This is thrown into sharp relief when Bell argues against perceptions of ritual that view it as a kind of "belief factory," wherein ritual is inherently comprehensible to its participants and yields predictable and controllable belief systems that depend on its rites and rubrics. In Bell's words, "Most symbolic action, even the basic symbols of a community's ritual life, can be very unclear to participants or interpreted by them in very dissimilar ways."[40] Such dissimilar work of interpretation by members of the community who participate in the community's rituals bespeaks the unpredictability of the structural elaboration phase of Archer's morphogenetic cycle. The helix of morphogenesis tilts in one way or another in response to the practices (read: social interactions) of a community, including ritual, but it does not do so in obedience only to the explicit power brokers of the community. The exercise of agency is alive and well in ritualization, but when agents act, the effects of that action may or may not be what they intend. The social machinery of ritualization does not manufacture reliable products as a factory; instead, the social structures and realities that emerge from the ritualization process carry meaning—do the work of symbolization—that moves beyond agents' intentionality. This is not a result simply of having insufficient social data or aptitude; it is a feature of the processes of both ritualization and the morphogenetic cycle. Keeping these resonances in mind (and, of course, being open to other emergent ones), we turn now to reading ritualization and the morphogenetic cycle out of examples drawn from rural contexts.

Now Part of the Ritual: The Sanctuary and the Service Dog

When my maternal grandfather was alive, he served in his retirement as something of a long-term interim minister and pastor for rural Christian congregations in North Dakota that were relatively local to

40. Bell, *Ritual Theory, Ritual Practice*, 183.

him and that sometimes had difficulty attracting and keeping full-time pastors. The reasons for this difficulty varied, from the financial stresses of providing a living wage to the pastor, to the scarcity of ministers willing or interested to wrestle with the climate of rural North Dakota, to the sparsity of certain amenities available in the communities, to church communities' insistence on hiring pastors who could sing well and would be willing to keep up rigorous pastoral care regimens that often included significant travel time. These and other facets of rural ministry made regular fodder for my grandfather's stories (he was a wonderful storyteller), who himself reveled in the aesthetics and practices of rural living. He gloried in the remoteness of his chosen home, a community with a population of roughly thirty persons, situated a twenty-five-minute drive away from the next larger city with a population of about sixteen hundred. He loved the tight-knit community life, both facilitated and demanded by the low-density population, which is the operative factor in this story from his experience.

One year a local congregation welcomed a new permanent pastor, which provided a measure of blessed respite for my grandfather. By most accounts, the pastor was a good fit, able to sense and respond to the liturgical tastes of the community, unperturbed by the drive time included in the position's responsibilities, and willing enough to endure the harsh North Dakota winters. As a side vocation, this pastor also trained service dogs, a sometimes demanding task that, for him, resonated with his call to ministry. Few in the community objected to this side vocation, though it was also the case that not many of the community had much experience with service dogs. Most of the animals the community was familiar with were farm-service animals, livestock, or pets.

All seemed relatively well until a group of parishioners—in a state of consternation and visible agitation—brought news to my grandfather that the new pastor allowed his service-dogs-in-training to eat on the carpet of the church's sanctuary during church services. Such a thing, they opined, betrayed a blatant lack of respect for the community, its piety, and its resources. For context, the carpet was relatively new, having been replaced only a few years prior—a significant expenditure for the community, whose membership had been aging and declining in number. The community took deep offense to this, and it became part of a toxifying relationship that culminated in the pastor leaving the community (or being forced out, depending on how one reads the events). This, in turn, led to a resumption of my grandfather's ministerial duties and the continued process of working to call another permanent pastor.

To be clear, I never heard the pastor's side of this narrative, and that is part of the point. Neither the morphogenetic cycle nor the practice of ritualization includes any inherent tilt toward balance, justice, fairness, or equity. Each of those moral categories depends on the particular ways social realities and rituals develop and the agents involved in that development. From an outside perspective, the community's strong response against a service-dog-in-training eating during a church service may seem inappropriate or outsized (and my goal is not to indicate one way or the other). However, the point here is not simply about the community's reaction but instead about the ritual and structural makeup that made such a reaction possible or likely in the first place. The church's sanctuary in this case was not just a space where a community's worship services happened. It was a place steeped in the history of the community, kept open by the not-insignificant effort of persons with deep community roots, making real—symbolizing—church and community vitality even in the absence of a pastor. The structural and ritual role of pastor was a necessary one, but it was relativized by the community's necessary resilience in its absence. The structural conditioning of the community did not include significant deference to departures by the pastor from what was seen as the commonsense norm of church life. In a word, animals didn't eat on the church carpet, as that community saw it, and no amount of intellectual distinguishing between service-dogs-in-training and other animals prevented that structural aberration from having ritual—and social—effect. The dogs entered the ritual space, thereby becoming part of the symbolic structure of the ritual space and action; neither the pastor nor the community was completely free to determine as they wished the social impact of that practice. Neither the community nor the pastor seemed to harbor any ill intent, but this social misfire became a symbol that mediated more meaning than simply an eating dog. It ritualized a structural change for which the community and the pastor were unprepared.

Structures Only Matter If They Matter: Dollar General Comes to Town

A number of years ago, Dollar General built a store in the corner of the cornfield across the street from my home in my community with a population of roughly 1,700. The process of Dollar General acquiring the land and relevant building permits required a rezoning of the land from what was built into the city's strategic plan in order to accommodate Dollar General's commercial interest. It was a divisive and fairly rancorous process. Part of the community readily welcomed the arrival of Dollar General wherever it wanted to build—the only grocery store in town at the time was in the process of going out of business, and while Dollar General does not carry a full complement of grocery options, it did offer the possibility of keeping *some* grocery availability within the city limits. Other parts of the community objected to Dollar General's choice of location; the main street of the town had many vacant lots on which to build, but this new construction was slated for the outskirts of the town, away from both other main street businesses and accessibility infrastructure like sidewalks.

The points of interest for this discussion come from the city council meetings in which the rezoning was discussed (argued over) and approved. Small city councils generally do endeavor to run their meetings with some form of parliamentary procedure rules, and my hometown is no exception in this. However, it became clear quite quickly in the meetings associated with rezoning for Dollar General that the procedural rules were relative guidelines rather than structural absolutes. Discussion by community members, the Dollar General representative, and city council members regularly unfolded in the meetings regardless of whether the structural norms allowed for it, sometimes when explicitly called for and other times when someone simply had something to say. Arguments unfolded this way regarding whether the existing city road was built to accommodate the large trucks Dollar General uses for delivery, whether the placement of the driveway presented a hazard to children visiting the neighboring playground since there were no sidewalks, and whether rezoning was a good idea with so much commercial real estate already readily available in town.

Ultimately, the city ended up approving essentially everything Dollar General requested, much to the chagrin of a number of community residents, but the process by which it was done amounted to a fusion of official structural actions (council votes, etc.) with less-formalized practices by those attending those functions. If discussion was pronounced closed, and then someone or a group of people continued to discuss or debate, little if any structure was exercised to halt that discussion or debate until it organically concluded. Likewise, if evidence was presented (such as evidence that the existing street had *not* been built to accommodate large delivery trucks), its impact was relativized by the flow of conversation in what may have looked to an outside observer more like an open community forum. The point in this is that the rubrics of a structure practice—the city council meeting—held only limited sway over the exercise of community agency in the discernment of this rezoning. The limiting of that sway was not officialized in any way that I could see as a participant, except as a function of common sense, in the way that Bell refers to the term. The power to rezone part of the city's strategic plan was filtered through a set of structures governed at least as much by community sense and desire as it was by official process. As far as I could tell, this did not seem to present much of a problem for anyone involved; it was the way small towns like this operated.

Ritual Inclusion: A Farm Mass

The first year I facilitated a rural immersion program for graduate students at Saint John's School of Theology and Seminary, we were blessed to be invited to a "mass on the road,"[41] a celebration of Eucharist that took place in the evening, outdoors on a farm in one of the local parishes.

---

41. See Jeff Johnson, "'On the Road' Masses Are a Mingling of Creativity and the Holy Spirit," *Central Minnesota Catholic*, June 14, 2023, https://thecentralminnesotacatholic.org/on-the-road-masses-are-a-mingling-of-creativity-and-the-holy-spirit/.

It was a deeply Minnesotan outdoor experience, including a steady rain that slowly let up through the course of the mass and prolific mosquitoes that had no fear of the rain and were hardy enough to ignore most of our bug repellant. Beyond the physical outdoor characteristics, however, the liturgical community that came together and ritually reconstituted itself in the celebration of Eucharist was a welcoming and hospitable one. The priest who celebrated the mass took time prior to the celebration to talk with our students about his experience and perception of rural and small-town ministry, and the owners of the farm introduced us to the gathered community during their brief introduction to their home. The mass itself was beautiful, celebrated with enthusiastic music that most of the community knew by heart and with a core sense of reverence for both the rites and the setting, but it was what took place after the mass that illustrates well the interplay among structure, agency, and ritualization.

When the mass concluded, the community was invited to share a more substantial meal: The farm owners had made a large amount of hardy soup, a local bakery had donated plenty of fresh sourdough, and beverages of all kinds abounded. This act of hospitality did not distinguish between visitors and community members; as I and my students ate and chatted with folks, it became clear that something more than refreshment was taking place. I do not wish to sentimentalize the hospitality of the community or the hosts, but when I finally was able to drag the students back to the bus and return to campus several hours later, we were still among the first to leave. The community took fellowship quite seriously, and while it was not officially connected to the celebration of mass, its organic continuation of the spirit of welcome and belonging was palpable, sustaining itself well into the evening after the official ritual had concluded.

The fellowship that followed mass was supported by a certain loose set of structures (hosts—community—visitors), but the interplay among the individual agencies of those participating and the combined communal agency of the assembly to actually *do* fellowship precipitated a social practice that emerged beyond the makeup of its constitutive elements. *That* folks ate and talked with each other is not necessarily remarkable; the *way* they did so elaborated the social structures in a way that built up and edified many who participated. When students reflected on the experience, they did more than just report that they learned about particular community members' lives and experiences (though they did that as well). They wrestled with *meanings* that took shape as a result of their interactions. As Bell suggests, the ritualization of this hospitality birthed varied and dissimilar interpretations—some students focused on feelings of welcome, others on the country aesthetic, others on what it meant to share food, and others on the meaning of being together through the rain and bugs—but those interpretations moved beyond the empirical into the symbolic. Sharing non-ritual food and drink after participating in the ritual meal of the Eucharist nevertheless took on a ritual character, sustained by a social reality whose roots ran deeper than what was externally observable.

My goal in relating these stories is, again, not to give a kind of paternalistic interpretation of what somehow *really* took place. Instead, these serve as illustrations of how critical realist sociology and Bell's approach to ritual theory interact and yield a stage set for a more in-depth and intentional engagement with the concept of symbol, which is the subject of the next chapter. Having now laid out what is connoted by "the rural" and how social structures and ritualization develop and progress, our discussion can turn in earnest to the symbolic depth of social reality and its relationship to social ethics.

CHAPTER THREE

Symbolization in Sacramental Theology and Social Ethics

Introduction: An Unhelpful Dichotomy

IN POPULAR PARLANCE, speaking of something—especially an action—as "symbolic" tends to suggest that it is empty of any real meaning or power. What is real or effective is often thought of as opposed to, or at least separate from, the realm of the symbolic. An action may be reduced to something "largely symbolic" when it fails to hold the power necessary to do something *more* than symbolize, and an object may be symbolic in that it holds sentimental meaning, is emblematic, or operates as a shorthand for something that one can easily interpret if one possesses the correct key of references. In such a perspective, what is real is reduced to what can be described, defined, and effectively manipulated to produce a particular desired outcome. The symbolic then becomes a servant of the real, a method of pointing toward the real or reflecting the real but not participating in the real in a proper sense. Symbol becomes derivative and accidental rather than primary and essential.

This kind of perspective—widespread especially in the West—could be blamed on any number of intellectual and cultural factors: the residue of the Enlightenment, another facet of the technocratic paradigm, a twisting of scientific method, empiricism's unfortunate implication, and so on. Against this backdrop, however, a number of theological disciplines have undertaken to correct or clarify what a symbol is and how the symbolic order functions. Symbol is an essential category for Christianity, and a great deal is at stake in understanding or misconstruing it. Within systematic theology, probably the most influential work on symbol in recent decades has sprung from Karl Rahner's foundational treatment of the subject.[1] Such work is very valuable, but for the purposes of this project, sacramental theology contains the most helpful theological treatments of symbol, especially the work of Louis-Marie Chauvet and those who have taken inspiration from him.[2]

Sacramental theology, along with its partner liturgical theology, is particularly helpful for understanding the social-ethical role of symbols and their operation because its culmination, its *telos*, is not simply theological understanding but religious practice. Sacramental and liturgical theology are not ordered only toward comprehension of what takes place when sacraments and liturgy are celebrated; the celebration itself is primary. Put a different way, discourse *about* what is going on in Christian ritual is secondary to what actually *is* going on in Christian ritual.[3] Such an alignment of the academic discipline invites practical discourse regarding how the celebration of Christian ritual embodies (or not) Christian ethics.[4] Wider than that, since Christian practice of liturgy

---

1. Karl Rahner, "The Theology of the Symbol," in *Theological Investigations*, vol. 5, trans. Karl-H Kruger (Seabury, 1974), 42–66. See also Rhodora E. Beaton, *Embodied Words, Spoken Signs: Sacramentality and the Word in Rahner and Chauvet* (Fortress, 2014), and Stephen M. Fields, *Being as Symbol: On the Origins and Development of Karl Rahner's Metaphysics* (Georgetown University, 2000).

2. Beyond Chauvet, *Symbol and Sacrament*, see Chauvet's more approachable book *The Sacraments: Word of God at the Mercy of the Body* (Liturgical Press, 2001), as well as Bruce Morrill, *Divine Worship and Human Healing: Liturgical Theology at the Margins of Life and Death* (Liturgical Press, 2009), or Lizette Larson-Miller, *Sacramentality Renewed: Contemporary Conversations in Sacramental Theology* (Liturgical Press, 2016), and the essays in Philippe Bourdeyne and Bruce T. Morrill, eds., *Sacraments: Revelation of the Humanity of God* (Liturgical Press, 2008).

3. See Aiden Kavanaugh's classic distinction between primary and secondary liturgical theology in Aiden Kavanaugh, *On Liturgical Theology* (Liturgical Press, 1984).

4. This is a growing area of scholarship. See, for example, Layla Karst, "Caught in the Act: Karl Rahner, Brian Flanagan, and the Problem of Liturgical Failure," *Horizons* 50, no. 1 (2023): 32–61; Benjamin Durheim, "Just Liturgy: Connecting Theological Ethics and Liturgical Practice," *Proceedings of the North American Academy of Liturgy* 2018 (2018): 79–93; or David Turnbloom, "Liturgy in the Shadow of Trauma," *Religions* 13, no. 7 (2022): 583, https://doi.org/10.3390/rel13070583.

and sacraments is a central part of crafting and recrafting Christian individual and ecclesial identity, engaging the ways ritual practice does so provides a baseline for understanding how ritual—both religious and not—impacts social identity and the governing ethics thereof, especially in contexts such as rural America, where Christianity has significant voice and influence.[5]

Such attention to the relationship between ritual and identity is one reason Chauvet's work is particularly helpful. For Chauvet, to conceive of Christian identity apart from liturgical/sacramental practice borders on the nonsensical;[6] it is from the ritual milieu of Christianity that the church and its members derive the very language (a loaded term for him) that speaks Christian approaches to truth, beauty, and goodness. Further, one of Chauvet's foundational concerns when he constructs his sacramental theology is to depart to some degree from deterministic, instrumentalist understandings of causality: presumptions that an action must have definable, predictable, controllable effects. Frustrated by what he saw as overly mechanistic approaches to Christian ritual, Chauvet turns instead to the paradigm of gift-giving, reinterpreting it not as a misapprehension of social practice (recall the example from Bourdieu and Derrida in chapter 2) but as a fundamental way of being that differs from more mechanistic operations like market exchange. Doing so allows Chauvet to dodge the unhelpful dichotomy of symbol versus real and instead describe poles of language and identity between which there is a spectrum: sign on the one side and symbol on the other. Every social action for him is suffused with both, and fully grasping ecclesial and social reality requires a literacy in both.

To engage Chauvet's conception of symbol and draw implications for social reality and ethics, the chapter begins by outlining Chauvet's

5. Recall that 73–83 percent of rural residents in the United States identify as Christian (Public Religion Research Institute and American Communities Project Staff, "Religious Stereotypes vs. Reality in Urban, Suburban, and Rural America").

6. See Louis-Marie Chauvet, "The Liturgy in Its Symbolic Space," in *Liturgy and the Body*, eds. Louis-Marie Chauvet and Francois Kabasele Lumbala (Orbis, 1995), 29–40.

objections to philosophical and theological overreliance on categories of causality and metaphysics, as well as his understanding of language and social identity that serves to correct it. This includes a basic definition of what Chauvet means by "symbol," as well as the operation of the symbolic order—a process by which reality is mediated to those who experience it. Subsequently, the chapter turns to what Chauvet calls "symbolic exchange," by which he essentially means gift-giving. This sets the necessary architecture for reckoning with the symbolic order in social reality, particularly in relationship with exercises of agency and the unpredictability of emergent social structures (this builds on the engagement of critical realist sociology from chapter 2). Third, based on Chauvet's understanding of symbol, the chapter moves to a more explicit description of how symbol and social ethics mutually inform. Essential in this analysis is the role of the body—individual and social—and its ritual and linguistic makeup. Finally, the chapter concludes with a treatment of what might be called *symbolic literacy*—the ability to interpret symbols not as reducible to packets of discursive content but as distinct mediations of social reality—and how such literacy has been inculcated in Christianity in liturgical and sacramental practice. Having laid all this out, this first part of the book closes, making way for Part II, which explores particular ways the symbolic order underwrites social reality in rural America.

What Symbol Isn't: Sign and Instrument

Chauvet, a French Catholic priest, did something in the last part of the twentieth century that was rather theologically risky: He crafted a critique of Thomas Aquinas, and built his sacramental theology on a conviction that it would be helpful to do something *other* than Thomistic sacramental theology. His goal was to provide a corrective against using Thomas's theological system to mechanize Christian liturgical and sacramental practice. The impact of Thomas Aquinas's theology on Roman Catholic theology in particular, and sacramental theology more generally, can hardly be overstated. Thomas's theology swims under nearly every official Roman Catholic document related to sacramental theology and practice. His work provides both inspiration for and (occasionally) something to oppose for protestant approaches to sacramental and liturgical theology, and the breadth of his theological thought, along with its sometimes dogged coherence, has earned him a privileged spot in nearly every corner of theological inquiry.

Against this backdrop of nearly universal latent Thomism, Chauvet objected to what he saw as a peculiar fixation endemic in the medieval theological context of which Thomas was a part: a significant focus on the operation of causality, particularly in terms of instrumental causality.[7] Sacraments are not simply representations or performances; sacraments *do* things. Specifically, the sacraments are ways by which Christians receive and participate in grace—God's presence and action—which begs the question of exactly *how* they do so. Addressing this question, in Chauvet's mind, is a central orientation of sacramental theology; as he argues, "We cannot make sense of the sacraments if we attempt to start from rational deductions. We are simply trying to understand what we *already* believe, immersed as we are . . . in *sacramentality*."[8] The basic content of "what we already believe" with regard to the operation of sacraments, for Chauvet, is summed up in "the old Scholastic adage according to which the sacraments . . . 'effect what they represent' (*efficunt quod figurant*)."[9] This is, of course, far too broad of a brush with which to paint the whole of Christian sacramental theological inquiry, but it points out Chauvet's central concern—and resonates deeply with this current discussion. How Christians think something happens in the sacraments is just as important as what they think is happening in the first place—and this is the rub.

In Chauvet's reading, which has not gone unchallenged,[10] Thomas's view of how sacraments effect what they represent is dependent on a

7. Chauvet, *Symbol and Sacrament*, 16.

8. Chauvet, *Symbol and Sacrament*, 2. Emphases in original.

9. Chauvet, *Symbol and Sacrament*, 17.

10. See, for example, Joseph C. Mudd, *Eucharist as Meaning: Critical Metaphysics and Contemporary Sacramental Theology* (Liturgical Press, 2014).

conceptual marriage of causality and signification, which is in turn dependent on Greek metaphysics.[11] To *cause* is not necessarily a problem; to cause by *signifying* presents a significant conceptual challenge because it requires "harmonizing two categories as completely foreign to one another as are 'sign' and 'cause,' and doing so in such a way that the type of sign under examination would have these unique traits: it would indicate what it is causing and it would have no other way of causing except by the mode of signification."[12] For example, consider how a stop sign causes cars to stop. The stop sign signifies a directive—that one should stop here—but then that signification is filtered through other actions (the driver's comprehension, the action of engaging the car's brakes, the operation of the brakes on the velocity of the car as it stops, etc.) that cause the car to stop. The stop sign causes cars to stop not by its own signification itself but by the reception of that signification by other agents and their consequent actions. Sign and cause are separate in the case of the stop sign. Imagine, however, if the stop sign, *simply by signifying what it does (the directive to stop)*, caused cars to stop without separate action from drivers and mechanical causes within the cars. That is the conceptual marriage of cause and signification that Chauvet sees Thomas working toward.

To be clear, Chauvet's goal was never to throw Thomas out. In fact, Chauvet's resistance to the Thomistic understanding of sacraments is not principally due to the difficulty of marrying sign to cause in sacramental practice.[13] Instead, Chauvet's problem is with signification itself and the stranglehold he thinks it has on Christian understandings of sacramentality. In essence, Chauvet thinks that Thomas ultimately works to "subordinate the notion of causality to that of sign,"[14] blocking out any other possible way of understanding how sacramental

11. Chauvet, *Symbol and Sacrament*, 16–36.

12. Chauvet, *Symbol and Sacrament*, 17–18. Emphases removed.

13. Chauvet actually praises Thomas's insights in doing so. See Chauvet, *Symbol and Sacrament*, 18.

14. Chauvet, *Symbol and Sacrament*, 12. Emphasis removed.

causality functions. This hegemony, for Chauvet, effectively elevates a Greek metaphysical way of thinking and speaking to indubitability, epistemologically stunting sacramental theology and rendering it less capable of adequately interfacing with contexts that are no longer that of medieval Europe. The reason for this is bound up in what a sign actually is, what signification means, and the way these concepts govern human understandings of reality.

Thus far I've resisted laying out a quick and easy definition of sign or signification because the problems Chauvet sees with their hegemony are root-level problems, not simply definitional ones. Substantively, a sign is something that conveys information or content, and signifying is the process of conveying that content. In Chauvet's view, drawing significantly from Heidegger,[15] the epistemological stranglehold of sign is built directly into the operative view of human language that has largely governed how metaphysics is done in the West—the view of human language as instrument: "Rather than considering language as the 'mutual belonging together' (*Zusammengehörigkeit*) of 'Being' (*Sein*) and the 'human being' (*Dasein*), the metaphysical tradition views language as belonging exclusively to humans. An 'animal having language' (*zoon logon echon*), a 'rational animal' (*animal rationale*), the human being is an entity that has, among other *attributes*, speech."[16] In this view, the primary function of language is to express intellectual or cognitive content, to verbalize thoughts. The process of doing so is stepwise: *First* a person has a thought, *then* the person finds the relevant instruments (words) to give voice to that thought, and *finally* the person expresses the thought in language. Conceived in this way, human beings are masters of language and may use it to produce whatever meanings they wish, as long as their audience is sufficiently trained in the similar use of the tools of language.

15. Chauvet, *Symbol and Sacrament*, 26–32. See also Martin Heidegger, *Identity and Difference*, trans. Joan Stambaugh (University of Chicago, 2002), and Martin Heidegger, "Letter on 'Humanism,'" in *Martin Heidegger: Pathmarks*, ed. William McNeill (Cambridge University, 1998), 239–276.

16. Chauvet, *Symbol and Sacrament*, 33. Emphasis in original.

Admittedly, for many people much of the time, this view of language may be nearly self-evident. If I am in an unfamiliar place and want to know where the restroom is, all I want is for a person or signage to indicate to me the relevant information about where the nearest restroom can be found. If I'm searching for instructions online for how to replace a light fixture, I want the source that most efficiently distills that information into content that I can comprehend quickly and easily so I can get to the actual work of replacing the fixture. And I vividly recall having the deeply relieving experience I suspect many parents have, of my children finally growing into the ability to wield the language instrument to express in intelligible terms their responses to questions like "what hurts?" or "what's wrong?" or "why did you do that?" All this is to say that using language as an instrument is not inherently some terrible thing. It's not even necessarily false. What it is, for Chauvet, is *incomplete*, and as such its falsehood only grows by the extent to which it is allowed to monopolize our understanding of how language functions.

Metaphysics depends on language. What we *say* exists is inseparable from *how* we say what exists. Language is how humans access reality, even at its most fundamental level; in Chauvet's words, "There is no human reality, however interior or intimate, except through the mediation of language or quasi-language that gives it a body by expressing it."[17] Accordingly, if humans are masters of language—if they are outside of language itself and are free to use language simply as an instrument—then what is *real* becomes simply what is *produced*. Instruments and tools exist for a purpose; they exist in order to accomplish something. If language is an instrument, then it exists in order to accomplish or produce, not to simply exist without a technical purpose. Consequently, for Chauvet, since this perspective of language largely governs metaphysics, any conception of a thing that exists tends to be constructed in terms of its purpose or productivity. Simply to *be* is nearly nonsensical; to *be* is to cause something, produce something, pursue something. This is the problem that Chauvet reads

17. Chauvet, *Symbol and Sacrament*, 90. Emphasis removed.

out of Thomas's sacramental theology: Causality is subsumed under signification—language as instrument. In his words, commenting on Thomas's explanations of sacramental efficacy, "Sacraments '*cause* grace,' they '*work*' or '*produce*' it, they '*contain*' it, they '*add to*' grace . . . they '*confer*' grace, they derive their '*virtue of producing* [causativa] *grace*' from the Passion of Christ. The whole question is conceived according to the model of an '*instrument*.'"[18] Of course, Chauvet notes that all this is for Thomas by way of analogy, but he argues that "even when purified by the reminder that it is only an analogy, these terms all serve to build up a never-present scheme of representation that we call technical or productionist."[19] Sacramental reality, when subjected to a monopoly of signification over the operation of language and metaphysics, risks reduction to instrumentalization.

The epistemologically fatal flaw in this conception of language and metaphysics is the operative but illusory conviction that all essential meaning, in the final account, can be expressed by means of instruments over which humans exert mastery. In living as if this were the case, humans short-circuit their understanding and appreciation of the depth of the realities they inhabit (natural, social, political, religious, and otherwise), leading to shortcomings not necessarily of intention but of apprehension. If language is no more than an instrument of production, then the realities humans craft for themselves will at best be phantasms, cheap simulacra exhibiting only pale reflections of the deep richness that can be accessed only by stepping outside of sign's epistemological prison. *How* to step outside is the question, and Chauvet's resounding answer is to begin by recognizing another concurrent way of conceiving of reality and language: not sign but symbol.

For Chauvet, if sign monopolizes language when language is viewed as an instrument, then breaking that monopoly requires a *non*instrumentalist view of language. This, too, Chauvet draws from

18. Chauvet, *Symbol and Sacrament*, 21. Emphases in original.

19. Chauvet, *Symbol and Sacrament*, 22. Emphases removed.

Heidegger (along with Levinas),[20] but his concern is ultimately theological rather than philosophical. What it means to conceive of language as noninstrumental is to recognize that language speaks humans, not the other way around. By this I don't mean that human bodies don't physically exist until language takes place but rather that when language *does* take place, there is nearly always *more* that is conveyed than simply information. To return to an example from above, when in an unfamiliar place I ask someone where I can find the restroom, the person's response *both* conveys information *and* establishes a kind of relationship. If the person responds in a friendly manner, I receive not just directions to the bathroom but also an indication that *who I am* in this space is not "unwelcome stranger" but "agreeable newcomer." That identity is added on to all the other identities I bring with me, becoming part of a world that linguistically precedes and transcends me. *How* did I perceive that my conversation partner responded in a friendly manner? Any satisfactory answer to this question resists reduction to packets of information accessible through body language, voice inflection, and the like. There is *more*. There is a whole—a world of meaning, implication, and mediation—to which I and my partner have access not discursively but by virtue of the fact we have been formed by the life of that whole, in total and in the operation of all its distinct parts. *This* is the symbolic order. It is the mediation of relational and social reality through means that are not reducible to data delivery and interpretation. Symbol is the *more* that makes sign information itself identifiable as distinct from what is beyond simply raw information.

It is important to note at this point that both sign and symbol are nearly always operative in the human exercise of language. In this Chauvet argues that they are not two *kinds* of language or two *models* of language but two *poles* of language.[21] Particular exchanges of language unfold somewhere along the continuum between these two poles,

20. Chauvet, *Symbol and Sacrament*, 55, 90. See also Emmanuel Levinas, *Totality and Infinity: An Essay on Exteriority*, trans. Alphonso Lingus (Kluwer Academic, 1991).

21. Chauvet, *Symbol and Sacrament*, 111.

at times emphasizing information transfer while minimizing identity mediation and at other times emphasizing identity mediation and minimizing information transfer. It is not necessary (or advisable) to fantasize about inhabiting a *purely* noninstrumental logic of language, but in order to more fully access and account for the realities humans inhabit, it is necessary to relativize the epistemological weight of signification and also recognize the weight of the symbolic order. In a world of shared social reality, the concept of symbol is essential for reckoning with one's experience of the world, its social-ethical makeup, and the role one plays within it. Symbol is communally constituted; "it is the expression of a social pact based on mutual recognition . . . a mediator of identity."[22] To understand symbol is to access a way into viewing the depth of social reality that does not reduce language and existence to instrument and production. To access symbolic reality is to access human reality.

Much of this section has served to indicate what symbol is *not* rather than what it is. Such was my attempt to keep signification from slipping behind the trappings of symbol and masquerading as more than it is. Having done this, the conversation can now move more explicitly to how symbol and symbolization function in Chauvet's view and the central differences between their operative logic and that of sign: their relationship to value and gift and their dependence on action.

What Symbol Is: Mediation, Action, Nonvalue

Taken together, the poles of sign and symbol constitute a human experience of language within which, for Chauvet, human life emerges from experiences of raw sensation toward full, socially mediated perceptions. Along with the illusory monopoly of sign over language and causality, there is another popularly operative falsehood about language and identity that Chauvet is eager to shed: the temptation of immediacy. Too often, people operate as if they have immediate intellectual access to the fullness of the realities they encounter, leading—much like the problems with overinflated emphases on signification—to false certainties

22. Chauvet, *Symbol and Sacrament*, 112.

regarding what are perceived as facts and situations. In an example Chauvet gives, "between sensation and perception there is a margin: the stone that violently hits the head provokes an identical *sensation* of pain in the animal and in the human being, but the *perception* of the stone is of another order."[23] The stone, within human language and experience, carries more than simply its physical weight. Perhaps the person subsequently kicks the stone away in annoyance, revealing a perception of the stone as malicious or simply unwelcome; or perhaps the person is spurred by the occasion to pause and reflect, not unlike Newton's apple; or any other of the endless possibilities of perceiving the stone. The point is that while the pain is immediate, the *cause* of that pain emerges, in the critical realist sense of becoming a higher order, not reducible to its constituent parts, as perception that is necessarily mediated by language. As such, it is filtered through the social constructions, cultural connotations, and personal histories of the one doing the perceiving. The object is then *not* simply fact or raw reality: "The perceived object is always-already a constructed object."[24]

Chauvet's insistence on this space between sensation and perception is less ideological than it is phenomenological. Considering experiences of reality—especially social reality—that are colored by everything from one's mood to one's family to one's social situation, it is not difficult to suggest that there is a space between what *is* and what is *perceived*. Chauvet calls this the "presence of the absence,"[25] by which he means there is something of a void that remains in any human perception. There is always more that is either missed or fades into the background due to any number of socially constituted factors that impact perception. Still, *any* human presence to an experience depends on the mediation of language, which for Chauvet does not mean only spoken-word language but additionally any method of giving a form of

23. Chauvet, *Symbol and Sacrament*, 85.

24. Chauvet, *Symbol and Sacrament*, 85. Emphasis removed.

25. Chauvet, *Symbol and Sacrament*, 98–99.

recognition or expression to a reality.[26] In this view, humans only ever have an incomplete picture of the realities they inhabit, a picture painted by the mediation of language.

Symbolization, then, operates as a kind of engine for mediation in human language exercise, where its complementary pole (sign) strives to deny the presence of the absence. Signification tends to pull toward the illusion of immediacy—what you see is what you get, and it can be named according to the instrument of language—and it is symbol that brings to bear both the recognition that there is distance between the human perceiver and what is perceived and the process of mediating perception across that distance. If this is the case, then it is necessary to consider what the symbolic order consists of in the first place. In a word, the answer for Chauvet is that the symbolic order is that of the body, both individual and social. More than simply receptive of sensation, the human body also speaks, not in vocalization only but in its very flesh. Who I am is bounded and expressed in a certain sense by the corporality of my body. As my body shifts and changes, it speaks both the same me and a changed me, given voice in my physical existence, inclusive of those parts inside me like my mind. The body localizes who I am and, by its very distinction from other bodies, emphasizes the irreducible space between the reality of me and the perception of me by others, the presence of my absence. Even when I am fully present to a person, group, or situation, I am not *immediately* present; my presence is mediated bodily, concomitant with an absence born of the simple fact that there is more to me than those to whom I am present can perceive. In this way, human existence is steeped in the symbolic; the body itself is a kind of primary symbol—as Chauvet calls it, the "arch-symbol."[27]

To be clear, this in no way means that a person's identity can be reduced to externally -visible attributes of their body. The body speaks, but it does not speak everything; it does not provide immediacy. My

---

26. He includes things like artistic expression, gesture, mime, and a host of other not quite linguistic expressions as part of what he means by "language" (Chauvet, *Symbol and Sacrament*, 87, no. 8).

27. Chauvet, *Symbol and Sacrament*, 151–152.

body's scars and characteristics are part of me and part of speaking me to the world I inhabit, but they are not all that I am. Instead, the individual body as arch-symbol speaks in a chorus of other symbol bodies that build up human identity and existence. These other bodies are shared bodies, communal bodies in which my own body participates and from which I derive large parts of who I am and how I live. Chauvet organizes these shared bodies into three: the body of society, which connotes the present community and context of which I am a part; the body of tradition or ancestry, which points to the shared histories that gave rise to the current context; and the cosmic body, which is the universe and environment within which the other bodies also live.[28] The import of this *triple body*, as Chauvet calls it, is that while the individual body connotes a space between who I am and what others perceive about me, the symbol of this shared triple body pulls at the space between my sense that I am an individual and the reality that my identity is more than my own; it has also been given to me by realities that precede and transcend me.[29]

Chauvet's connection of the symbolic order to the mediation of individual and social bodies introduces an essential consideration regarding the relationship of the symbolic order to perceptions of value. Symbol, in Chauvet's view, is distinct from sign in more than just its modality; it is also distinct in its relation to value and production. Put succinctly, if there is always *more* to human reality than what is perceived (i.e., symbol's pull toward the presence of the absence), then accurately assigning values to shards of that reality becomes a dicey business. Sign is tied to definition, and thereby instrumentalization and production, but if its complementary pole—that of symbol—is truly to be distinct from sign, symbol must resist instrumentalization, productionism, and the correlative necessity of assigning value. If symbol functions in a noninstrumentalist scheme of language, then it must also function according to a system

28. Chauvet, *Symbol and Sacrament*, 149–150.

29. This also points to the everydayness of the aspect of symbol. See also, for example, Jill Y. Crainshaw, *When I in Awesome Wonder: Liturgy Distilled from Daily Life* (Liturgical Press, 2017).

of non-value. This is not to say that symbols have *no* value; rather, value in terms of market exchange is irrelevant to the symbolic order. Symbol does not foreground objects that can be valued but instead subjects who are "beyond value."[30] Bodily mediation, both individual and communal, is the primary mode of the symbolic order, and the bodies of persons and communities resist assignment of market value. To define human persons or communities in terms only of market value is deeply *in*human.

This aspect of symbolic non-value takes clearer shape if one focuses less on symbol as a noun and more on the process of symbolization as a verb. Similar to the way Bell speaks of ritual in terms of the practice of ritualization, Chauvet's interest in symbol unfolds more as attention to human interaction that has symbolic depth rather than attempting to uncover the meaning of particular symbols. Accordingly, the practice of symbolic action—of symbolization—is more fertile for our purposes than trying to derive a multivalent key by which to interpret symbolic objects. To refocus on symbolic action is to shift the focus ultimately to the root of what makes the symbol symbolic, distinct from sign and value. In Chauvet's words, to approach a human interaction as symbolic "is to become primarily interested, not in the thing enunciated and in its value but in the *enunciation* and in the subject who through the enunciation speaks itself to another subject."[31] To wit, symbol is more a process than a thing. Symbolization unfolds as a practice within which the primary meaning is on the level of identity formation and exchange.[32]

For example, imagine you are invited to a dinner party. You might ask the hosts if you can bring anything to contribute to the meal, and if they say no, in many contexts you are generally free to show up with only yourself and some willingness to engage in good conversation. However, imagine you decide to bring a little something along as a gift anyway—a bottle of wine, some flowers for the table, or something similar. The primary meaning of this contribution becomes not *what* you brought

30. Chauvet, *Symbol and Sacrament*, 121.

31. Chauvet, *Symbol and Sacrament*, 119. Emphasis in original.

32. Chauvet, *Symbol and Sacrament*, 128–135.

or its value—it would usually be in bad taste for the hosts to ask how much the wine cost or to comment on which kinds of flowers they may have preferred instead—but simply *whether* and *how* you brought it. In some social contexts, a gift like this may be expected, and its absence would indicate either ignorance of what it means to be a guest or an intentional slight by a well-informed guest. In other social contexts, the opposite may be true; bringing a gift may be seen as overly formal or even pretentious, but identically in this case, a deviation from expectation would mediate a relational meaning. This contextual meaning-making is not reducible to definitions on the level of signification and value, and focused as it is on the relational dynamics between hosts and guests, it includes the manner of the action. Did you give the gift graciously? Dismissively? Timidly? Resentfully? And how did those characteristics take on flesh in the interaction? Your gift in this case is outside the realm of value (even of objective definition since it could be wine, flowers, or just about anything else); the symbolic order finds voice in the practiced interaction of subjects, not the disinterested transfer of objects.

Chauvet calls this process of interaction between human subjects that moves beyond value *symbolic exchange*. Ultimately, this is his answer to the question of how to conceive of reality and causality without reducing them to signification or instrumentalization. The foundation of symbolic exchange lies in the insight that when two humans exchange anything—help, time, attention, physical things—in Chauvet's words, "the true objects being exchanged are the subjects themselves."[33] Being a theologian, Chauvet connects this foundation directly to the gratuitousness and graciousness of God's grace—the convictions that we receive our very selves as a gift, and such gifts, along with our responses to them, are beyond value calculation[34]—which cements the paradigm of symbolic exchange as the practice of gift-giving. The very concept of the gift has been the subject of more than a little inquiry in late modernity

33. Chauvet, *Symbol and Sacrament*, 106.

34. Chauvet, *Symbol and Sacrament*, 108–109.

and postmodernity,[35] but Chauvet's understanding of the gift as symbolic exchange constitutes something of a unique perspective in that it takes gift-giving as primary and real rather than a kind of aberration of or intentional departure from market exchange and value.

Recall that Bell's theory of ritual practice included the necessity of the practice misrecognizing what it is doing, the example for which was precisely gift-giving, drawn from Bourdieu. The embedded assumption for Bourdieu appears to be that the default mode of human social existence is one of market exchange, and while gift-giving misrecognizes that, what is *really* going on in gift exchange is the transfer of value from one entity to another. For Chauvet, the case is more the inverse: It is market exchange—signification and instrumentalization—that scrapes away the relational depth of symbolic exchange. When humans interact with each other, acts of symbolization are *always* unfolding even if the persons do not recognize them as such. In some cases this is obvious, such as when persons greet one another; the content and meaning of a greeting are often a negotiation of relationship and clarification of relational identity. In other cases it is less so, like ordering a coffee at a coffee shop, where market exchange appears primary but includes structurally denoted subject-to-subject interaction in which much more takes place. Simply asking someone whether they had a good or bad experience at the coffee shop can invite an avalanche of symbolic content that goes far beyond the exchange of money for coffee. Symbolic exchange is a primary mode of human social constitution.

Symbolization and Social Ethics

In one sense, a primary reason it is important to attend to symbolization within social ethics is the epistemological space it maintains between

35. See Derrida, *Given Time*, and Derrida, *The Gift of Death*, as well as (for example) Jean-Luc Marion, *Being Given: Toward a Phenomenology of Givenness* (Stanford University, 2002); John D. Caputo and Michael J. Scanlon, eds., *God, the Gift, and Postmodernism* (Indiana University, 1999); or Calvin O. Schrag, *God as Otherwise than Being: Towards a Semantics of the Gift* (Northwestern University, 2002). Within liturgical theology, see, for example, R. Kevin Seasoltz, *God's Gift Giving: In Christ and Through the Spirit* (Continuum, 2007).

social reality and perceptions thereof. It should be clear by now that my agenda in pushing for literacy of the symbolic order in the work of social ethics is more than just wishing folks would interpret particular symbols better. In a world where data and information are increasingly available, one by-product has been the massive proliferation of opinions (and pressures to form and hold them) that take shape as a result of "informing oneself" or "doing one's own research."[36] Accessing information with a critical eye and careful thought is a good and necessary thing, but if the social world of which we are a part is largely governed by the principles of market exchange, instrumentalization, and production—and one would be hard-pressed to maintain that this is not the case—such social monopoly of these characteristics of signification cannot but precipitate social-ethical misfires and mistakes. Without recognition of and attention to the symbolic order, one simply does not have access to an accurate or adequate picture of social reality. Further than that, the symbolic order *itself* does not promise a comprehensive vision of social reality—that is exactly the point. The irreducible space between social reality and perception cannot be resolved by accessing more information or better data, but it is always lived into by means of the symbolic order of human social existence, by the process of symbolization.

This space between is perhaps most clear in the case of intentionally symbolic social actions such as rituals. For Chauvet as for Bell, ritual involves a practice that is set apart from the everyday, even if such a practice reflects the everyday. Chauvet calls this *heterotopy*, or a symbolic rupture, and explains it as some level of difference or separation of ritual practice from other practices of life.[37] The very keeping of this distance is an act of symbolization, mediating a particular meaning to the community that practices the ritual. The implication that there is always more going on than meets the eye takes on flesh by the distinction between

36. Such epistemological individualism has been the subject of more than a little discussion in fields attempting to move epistemic trust back to a more communal social location; see, for example, Linda Trinkaus Zagzebski, *Epistemic Authority: A Theory of Trust, Authority, and Autonomy in Belief* (Oxford University, 2015).

37. Chauvet, *Symbol and Sacrament*, 330–331.

ritualized actions and other non-ritualized actions. Additionally, such ritual rupture acts as a check on the ritual community itself, guarding against the community collapsing the ritual's meaning into easily accessible and definable data rather than engaging the process of bodily mediation. The temptation to domesticate ritual, to make it less than it is in favor of an illusory definitional control over the ritual, is no less common in religious communities than is the temptation to reduce social reality to definable data in broader society. For Chauvet, this is the Christian "sacramental stumbling block,"[38] the recognition that immediate, disembodied access to God or one another is a fallacy. Instead, particular ritual practices (sacraments) are a privileged way of mediating participation in the life of God and one's religious community.

To be sure, a person or community can flatly deny the reality of this bodily mediation. It is not always popular to suggest that there is an unavoidable and impassible space between one's perception of those one loves and the reality of those one loves. It can often be easier, more comforting, to presume that one has an unshakable and utterly reliable immediate sense of social or religious reality. This, however, is untruth. For Chauvet and many sacramental theologians, Christian rituals like the sacraments are not unnecessary add-ons to the more *real* or *essential* content of Christian life summarized by discursive belief.[39] Sacraments are more than religious window dressing. They are a privileged way of undertaking the bodily mediation that is an integral part of faith's engagement with the divine and the community. Sacraments and rituals like them hold the space between what is real and what is perceived by mediating such perception through ritualized bodily action. For Christianity, this is necessary not simply to make faith somehow easier to understand or to illustrate the mysteries of faith; it runs to the very core conviction of Christianity, that in order to fully express Godself to humans, God *took on flesh*, becoming mediated by a particular physical

38. Chauvet, *Symbol and Sacrament*, 153.

39. See, for example, Anscar J. Chupungco, *What, Then, Is Liturgy?* (Liturgical Press, 2010), or Albert Gerhards and Benedikt Kranemann, *Introduction to the Study of Liturgy* (Liturgical Press, 2017), esp. chaps. 1 and 4.

body and the social bodies of which Jesus was a part. To access that reality is more than intellectual; it requires the symbolization inherent in bodily mediation.

Similarly, outside ritual practice, actions' symbolic depth moves beyond data interpretation to bodily mediation of truth, both individual and communal. To return to the example that opened the introduction to this book, where the farmer who accepted an aid payment in exchange for plowing under monetarily worthless crops, then vomited as he began the process of plowing, it is unlikely he set out with the knowledge that this action would cause him to vomit. It was an unwelcome and unpleasant task to undertake, but difficult tasks are not exactly uncommon in agrarian life. Instead, the action itself of destroying the crops brought with it a symbolic depth; its process of symbolization made manifest a bodily reality that may not have been predictable given the raw data of the story. Further, the symbolizing causes and effects in this case (the floods, the aid program, the destruction of the crops, vomiting) are not completely separable but cohere in a symbolized whole. Once done, vomiting in the field in this case is inseparable from plowing under the crops and taking the aid payment. The full social truth of that symbolizing action, to the degree that such truth is apprehensible, is mediated bodily through the action itself.

Similarly, it is insufficient to speak only of the objects involved with the action as symbols. Like all objects given voice in language, the tractor, the field, the plow, and the other objects involved do evoke some level of both poles of language (sign and symbol), but symbolization is in the action itself. Action bodily mediates the possible into the actual, writing and speaking symbols in the process of symbolization. To refocus on symbolization as a practice or process relieves some of the problem of reducing symbols to decontextualized vessels of meaning. If we were to speak only of the farmer's field as a symbol, we would sunder the field from the rich array of meanings it connotes for the one working it, diluting its symbolic potency significantly or even completely. As Chauvet notes, "It is the entire symbolic order to which it belongs . . . that a symbol evokes."[40] Missing or misunderstanding the symbolic order that surrounds a particular symbol changes or even destroys the symbol itself for the one misapprehending it. The symbol then becomes nonsensical, or artificially shallow, hollowed out of the meaning that gave vitality to its symbolization in the first place. In a word, the symbol is inaccessible except by mediation within the symbolic order of which it is a part.

Diluting a symbol's potency by decontextualizing it does not only obfuscate the truths that the symbol may mediate; doing so also secretes a toxic social by-product of misapprehension—not necessarily of meaning but of significance. I suspect we have all had experiences wherein we have seen something that we hold dear cheapened in the dismissive or prejudicial gaze of someone or some community unfamiliar with its preciousness. Such misapprehension can cause significant pain and harm, and when it is on the level of communities or the organizing structures of power that govern them, the stakes can be dangerously high. Part of the challenge, however, is that full contextualization of symbols is not simply a matter of adding more and more cultural objects and information to "fill out" the symbolic frame of reference. To do so keeps symbols on the surface level of social reality, missing the symbolic depth of that reality that is built by subjects, not objects. Contextualization is more like encounter,[41] an action or process wherein context comes alive by virtue of human interactions. The truths of symbols depend on the acts of symbolization that constitute them, acts that carry meaning (signified and symbolized) according to the social milieux within which they take place.

40. Chauvet, *Symbol and Sacrament*, 115.

41. Encounter was a central concept in the thought of Pope Francis as well; see, for example, Pope Francis, "For a Culture of Encounter," *L'Osservatore Romano*, Weekly ed. in English 38, September 23, 2016, https://www.vatican.va/content/francesco/en/cotidie/2016/documents/papa-francesco-cotidie_20160913_for-a-culture-of-encounter.html; or John C. Cavadini and Donald Wallenfang, eds., *Pope Francis and the Event of Encounter* (Pickwick, 2018).

Focused, then, on the actions and process of symbolization rather than on artificially isolating the concept of symbol itself, an important resonance emerges between symbolization and the morphogenetic cycle of critical realist sociology. Recall that social structures derive from social interactions (exercises of agency; actions) by individuals and communities, which are in turn conditioned by the structural systems that precede them. This maintains the distinction in critical realist sociology between structure and culture (culture being the artifacts and world of ideas within which a social context functions and structure being the organizing relationships and roles that give contour to the social context).[42] However, approaching symbol not as a noun but instead by the process of symbolization resists reducing symbols themselves to cultural artifacts, which would miss the symbolic depth of social reality. Instead, symbolization as a process or an action inserts it into the morphogenetic cycle of *structural* change, somewhere between and shared by the helical turns of social interaction and structural elaboration. Symbolization in this sense, conditioned as it is by social-bodily mediation, precipitates what might be called *protostructures*, social relations that have been made manifest but are in various stages of being accepted or rejected as authoritative.

For example, when Cramer speaks of rural consciousness as including a sense of being ignored or passed over by centers of political and economic power, that sense is not reducible to objective data collection and analysis, though she does include a chapter dedicated to those tasks. Instead, *stories*—accounts of lived experiences, encounters, and actions (or nonactions, which amount much to the same thing)—were the primary sources of this sense. Her interviews showcase this repeatedly; the perception of rural areas being ignored was built by the myriad actions and encounters that unfold in the continued relationship between rural and nonrural areas. Even her experience interviewing

42. For Archer's explanation of how culture intersects with structure within the morphogenetic cycle, see Archer, *Realist Social Theory*, 305–309. See also Margaret S. Archer, *Culture and Agency: The Place of Culture in Social Theory* (Cambridge University, 1996).

rural folks as someone who is not from a rural area precipitated encounters like this; she speaks of being made to feel like a stand-in for the nonrural, a symbolic human representative of the spaces that are objects of rural resentment.[43] The point here is that while the rural-nonrural relationship is not structuralized as such (rather, it takes on myriad structural forms in political, social, economic, and religious systems), symbolizing actions manifest protostructural relationships, which, given sufficient repetition and narrative attention, can drive structural elaboration. Symbolization is in this way a kind of social-structural gesture, which may dissipate if the emergent symbols do not find full expression in the social context but may also become social-structural if they resonate with and mutually buttress other similar gesturing.

A brief example from my own research in rural Christian communities may help. One of the summers, we interviewed an elderly woman who had been a founding member of her local small-town church. It was a newer church (relatively speaking: approximately forty years old), or at least significantly newer than the other more established church in town, and had been a mission church founded as a kind of exploration of whether there were sufficient local members of the denomination to sustain a liturgical community. The local community's population is about seven thousand. When we asked her what her experience has been like in a rural church, she responded nearly immediately that her church and community were not *really* rural. The community had a grocery store after all, she said, and had even built a health-care clinic some years back. Additionally, it was only about a twenty-minute drive from the nearest "big city" (a city of a little fewer than seventy thousand people), and that came with relatively easy access to what she saw as nonrural services. For her, ease of access to amenities symbolized a departure from the rural more than questions of population or housing density. That symbolization is quite common—it may even seem self-evident to some—which is exactly the point. There is no necessary structural decree that defines the rural as devoid of amenities. However, experiences of lacking access to needed or desired goods and services by rural folks have sufficiently

43. See Cramer, *The Politics of Resentment*, 31–34.

gestured toward a protostructure of the rural as lacking amenities; consequently, the presence and accessibility of things like grocery stores and health-care clinics *made* the community less rural in the mind of this interviewee. That is not a necessary conclusion. It is part of the symbolic depth of society's structuring the rural and nonrural.

Put differently (and perhaps awkwardly), symbolization structures structures. The unpredictability of structural elaboration, conditioned as it is in critical realist sociology by the concept of emergence, is less unpredictable if one reads symbolization as part of that process of emergence. The question of society's symbolic depth becomes less about which symbols are operative where and more about how social interactions produce meaning in particular social contexts. They do so both by the obvious, definable results that unfold by instrumental causality *and* by the process of symbolization, which in Chauvet's vision belongs to the realm of non-value, of gift-giving. The morphogenetic cycle of critical realist sociology, for all its significant advantages (and there are many, particularly in relation to social ethics), is still largely captive to the instrumentalizing view of causality that Chauvet critiques as monopolistic in Thomistic sacramental theology and Western metaphysics more generally. For critical realist sociology, social interaction—having sprung from structural conditioning—causes structural elaboration. That this process is emergent or even indeterminate does not change the mode of the operative causality. Rather than augment instrumental causality with another kind, critical realist sociology defaults to a kind of pragmatic agnosticism regarding structural elaboration—much can be known and predicted, and much cannot.

Augmenting an interpretation of the morphogenetic cycle with an understanding of causality inclusive of symbolization and symbolic exchange catalyzes a deeper, richer method of social-ethical analysis. In a word, such a move *humanizes* analysis of, and interaction with, social structures. If social ethics cannot take adequate account of the symbolic depth of the social realities it interrogates, it risks reducing the issues it attends to—along with the persons and communities affected by them—to mere problems to be solved in order to produce better outcomes. Of course, not all approaches to social ethics do this, but in relation to the rural, there is already a potent history of rural folks perceiving rural issues and communities as having been reduced by external centers of power, including those of academic influence, to problems for solving, places where it is needful to find instruments by which to efficiently produce a "better" rural—often one made in the image of those doing the analysis.[44] Without the humanizing character built into recognizing the symbolic depth of social reality, we risk emptying social reality of its meaning and approaching questions of social makeup from standpoints that are set up from the beginning to miss the mark, such as Conn's reduction of rural America to the question of "to what extent and to what end the rest of the country is obligated to subsidize low-density living."[45]

If we were to extract the totalizing hermeneutics of market exchange and instrumentalization from analysis of rural America, or any other social context for that matter, making room instead for analysis within a logic of non-value and gift, it would become clearer (or at least less befuddling) why apparently contradictory social realities can layer on top of one another and coexist in human communal life. It is true that many rural folks, including farmers, are generally suspicious of or openly hostile to what they see as meddling from outside forces like state and federal governments. It is also true that massive numbers of rural counties depend on state funding to function, to say nothing of the necessity of the farm bill to make American agriculture work. This is one specific example, but there are myriad others: Rural communities can celebrate and despair at the same time, they can exert political influence and still experience marginalization, they can be simultaneously welcoming and also embody inhospitality, they can be supportive and also judgmental, and on and on.

44. See, for example, Nicholas F. Jacobs and Daniel Shea, *The Rural Voter: The Politics of Place and the Disuniting of America* (Columbia University, 2023).

45. Conn, *The Lies of the Land*, 256.

These contradictory social realities are only incoherent if we remain oblivious to the symbolic depth of social reality mediated by individual and social human bodies. Human life itself embodies contradiction and ambiguity. It is only by departure from embodied human existence that systems and structures can operate efficiently without exception or aberration. In this sense, beyond the symbolizing character of social interaction, social structures themselves have symbolic depth. When one encounters a system of relations in a social context that appears congruent with those relations elsewhere (structures), the full symbolic order out of which those relations rise is relevant to how those structures function. For example, is the role of a pastor primarily lead administrator or liturgical servant? It may include both, but the particular structural conditioning that includes the answer for a specific community will have layers of symbolization folded into it that resist reduction to classifying them only as cultural artifacts. When structures change or shift, the symbolic effects radiate out like aftershocks from an earthquake. Symbolic depth is not an optional add-on to social analysis; it is an aspect of individual and human being in the world that holds sway, whether it is recognized or not. The question is whether we are adequately equipped to do so.

Conclusion: Symbols Teach Symbols

If we endeavor to take symbolization seriously in the makeup of social reality, a brief word is warranted about how to develop literacy regarding symbolization. Since I've been at pains to maintain that this is *not* merely the ability to accurately interpret particular symbols but rather a process of adequately reckoning with the symbolic depth of social contexts, a method for doing so runs to the very margins of disciplines like sociology, history, and political science. This is part of the reason that the works of Chauvet and Bell loom large in this project: To recognize symbolization, to say nothing of attempting to *do* it intentionally, requires actually practicing symbolizing acts. Much like a craft, as distinct from an art or a science, symbolization is something built into the body—social and individual—that practices it.

As with any craft, reading symbolization is something that takes practice and repetition. Entering a space that is intentionally suffused with symbolic content and meaning facilitates attunement to symbolic depth. However, just as there is no such thing as a generic symbol isolated from its context, neither is there such a practice as generic symbolizing action or space. Instead, particular contexts of symbolization instill symbolic literacy that is specific to that context, and it is by resonance, analogy, and human encounter—that is to say, by *symbolic exchange*—that such literacy may be applied to contexts beyond one's own. Ultimately, this is a receptive process more than an analytical one; symbolic exchange is about non-value and gift-giving, so to receive the gift of encountering an act of symbolization that runs beyond one's contextual ken does not lend itself well to immediate value judgments or prescriptive, instrumentalizing analysis (i.e., social problem-solving). Rather, one receives according to one's disposition to receive; the gift of symbolization can only be seen for what it is—a gift—if the logic of gift, that of non-value, takes hermeneutical precedence.

Part of what this means in relation to rural America is that reckoning with the symbols and processes of symbolization that unfold there is to engage some of the relevant explicitly symbol-rich aspects of rural American life. One of those aspects is Christianity—recall that nearly eight out of ten residents of rural America identify as Christian[46]—which makes the intersection between Christian theological ethics and Christian liturgical/sacramental theology particularly relevant for understanding rural American social reality. Unfortunately, neither of these disciplines has thus far produced extensive or systematic contextual engagement with rural America.[47] Symbolization and

46. Public Religion Research Institute and American Communities Project Staff, "Religious Stereotypes vs. Reality in Urban, Suburban, and Rural America."

47. With some notable exceptions; see, for example, the essays in Victor Klimoski and Lance Barker, eds., *Abundant Harvest: Essays on Rural Life and Ministry in Honor of Dean and Elsie Freudenberger* (Minnesota Consortium of Theological Schools, 2000), as well as those in Gilson Waldkoenig, "Liturgy in Rural Settings," special issue, *Liturgy* 32, no. 4 (2017): 1–62.

symbolic depth are not necessarily *more* common or impactful in rural contexts than nonrural ones, but the rural is a context in which the symbolic depth of social reality plays out relatively legibly—albeit not without contradiction, paradox, or ambiguity. In bringing the tools of Christian sacramental theology to bear on social-ethical analysis, this chapter has laid out a path to theorizing the symbolic depth of social reality. What remains is to move from the theoretical to the practice of reading and writing symbols in rural America. With regard to symbolization, doing it, analyzing it, theorizing it, and constructing it are all quite inseparable.

Practically speaking, learning symbolization in context can be as straightforward as participating in symbol-rich community actions. In the case of Christianity, this means learning to read liturgical and sacramental action as the full, symbolizing practices they are. By this, I do not mean to evoke the unhelpful dichotomy that opened this chapter, that somehow recognizing the symbolic reality of something empties it of "real" reality. Fully engaging the symbolic depth of liturgical and sacramental practice *fleshes out* their reality; it does not *hollow* it out. Admittedly, this takes more work than simply study. It takes participation and encounter because the goal moves beyond digestion of information. To reckon with the symbolic depth of social reality is to move into a process of *receiving* that social reality and the persons who make it up. Such reception can be a vulnerable experience, just as learning any craft carries a risk of doing it badly to start. Add to this the fact that symbolic depth carries no guarantee of being ethically safe or stable—in fact, examples abound to the contrary—and the process of reckoning with symbolic depth of one's social reality can be one with real risk. This kind of risk is paradigmatic of human encounter, however, and that is part of the point. Adequately engaging (as well as understanding and analyzing) human social contexts cannot with integrity retreat from the necessity of actually humanizing them. To do so requires a great many things, one of which this discussion has highlighted: the need to engage the symbolic depth and symbolizing processes of social reality.

While these brief gestures toward how to facilitate literacy in relation to symbolization, they remain just that: gestures. They are initial intellectual and pragmatic steps for moving from theory in symbol and symbolization to practice. Such closes the first part of this book and paves the way for the second, where the primary concern and goal are to map out particular ways that symbolic depth plays out in rural social reality: an account of rural aesthetics, an examination of ethically problematic or simply malevolent processes of symbolization, and the multifaceted symbolizing effects mediated by the hybridization of physical, local community with online or virtual community.

II

Rural Symbolization and Social Ethics

CHAPTER FOUR

Rural Aesthetics, Rural Solidarity

Introduction: Why Aesthetics?

When I was an undergraduate, our family hosted an exchange student from Germany. It was altogether a delightful experience, and she remains a close friend to me and my family to this day. That year we spent part of the Christmas season traveling from our rural Minnesota town with a population of roughly thirteen hundred to a gathering at my maternal grandparents' home, which as I mentioned earlier is situated in rural northern North Dakota, part of a town whose population is approximately thirty (actually the house itself is four miles outside that town, but such specificity might be splitting hairs). That part of North Dakota in the summertime can be a breathtaking place—assuming one survives the mosquitoes—with fields of canola blooming radiant yellow and flax in seas of blue-purple. There is a river valley that runs across that part of the state that boasts gorgeous views of natural beauty; the prairie meeting a clear summer sky is a sight to behold. In winter, however, that area's natural flavor can be a bit more of an acquired taste. It's cold, sometimes bitterly so (the average December temperature in North Dakota is 15.5°F, with the record December chill hitting -50°F),[1] and strong wind sweeping across the plains without much if anything to break it can be oppressive. Add to that the hefty regular snowfall and the difficulty of keeping roads plowed in areas of sparse population, and the result is one that calls for a certain kind of cold-weather hardiness and grit.

---

1. North Dakota State Climate Office, *North Dakota Monthly Climate Summary* 17, no. 12 (December 2023): 3, 5, https://www.ndsu.edu/fileadmin/ndsco/ndsco/December23climate_final.pdf.

This was where the family gathering was to be held, however, so into the rural northern North Dakota winterscape we brought our German guest, eager as we were for family time and celebration. It was a windy and snowy evening (and dark—sunset comes early in a North Dakota winter) when we got off the relative comfort of Interstate Highway 94 and drove north. It was not the kind of idyllic, calm snow that one might dream of as adding to the beauty of an imagined downhome country Christmas but instead a drifting, blowing corn snow that demanded extra attention simply to the task of staying on the road. As we drove through expanse after expanse of snow-covered fields interrupted only intermittently by small towns, our guest's resting expression became more and more incredulous. When we finally approached our destination, turning off the paved county road onto yet another gravel one drifted over with the wind-hardening snow—a turn accentuated by passing a long-abandoned shack standing on its own out in the middle of a field, where it seemed to be in the process of slowly falling apart—our exchange student turned to us and asked, only partially joking, "Why would anyone live out here?"

In the years since then, our then guest, now sister, has made a number of trips with us out to our grandparents' North Dakota home—though not all in winter—and it's become a fond family memory to collectively recall that first trip in the snowstorm and the dark. I relate this brief vignette to introduce something of which many folks already have an intuition: that aesthetics and the tastes associated with it—our senses of what we find beautiful or moving—are not necessarily self-evident and certainly not universal. To look into the rural North Dakota snowstorm and see beauty is a far cry from being led to ask what could possibly tempt someone to live there (and, of course, even those who do live there may not choose *beautiful* as their first word to describe a December snowstorm). Beauty can be a difficult category to navigate, and aesthetic experience is not always a straightforward thing to analyze, but an account of symbol and social reality demands an earnest, if all too brief, treatment of aesthetics. That said, my goal is not to reduce aesthetics to a kind of "beauty is in the eye of the beholder" shallowness. Rather, situated as it is at the juncture between structure (social relations) and culture (social intelligibilia), aesthetics is a privileged vantage point from which to study a contextual perspective or set of perspectives. What is regarded as beautiful is often quite close to what is regarded as worthy, or of value, or illuminative. Put into the classic scheme of the three transcendentals of truth, goodness, and beauty, aesthetics is an indispensable piece of understanding the real, including social reality.

Part of the reason for this needful turn to aesthetics is that aesthetic sensibilities catalyze or inhibit the process of symbolization, according to the resonance or dissonance between the symbolizing act and those whose individual and social bodies mediate its meaning. If the "stuff" of an action speaks in and evokes well the linguistic milieu of the context in which it takes place and does so in ways that the social context can receive as aesthetically poignant, the potential meaning of that action extends quite quickly into symbolization. Conversely, if the stuff of an action is unfamiliar or unintelligible in a social context, its ability to interact with aesthetic sensibilities of the context is stunted, and symbolization is either slow or impossible. The point in this is that whether or not an action precipitates an explicitly aesthetic experience, aesthetic sensibilities nevertheless participate in the interpretation of any social action or reality. The question is often more a matter of how and to what degree.

The specific aim of this chapter is to sketch an outline of rural aesthetics in America in conversation with theological ethics and particularly the work of Nichole Flores, whose thought on what she calls *aesthetic solidarity* provides a framework for this chapter's contextual approach to rural aesthetics. The first part of this chapter lays out Flores's framework, relevant to this project both because of its contextual methodology and because of the way she connects aesthetics not simply to individual ethical discernment but also to the social concepts of solidarity and the common good. Following this, the chapter moves to giving an account of rural aesthetics based on my own research in rural

Christian communities in conversation with other sources.[2] Part of the difficulty in this section of the chapter is navigating the distinction but not separation between nonrural narratives and sensibilities *about* the rural, on the one hand, and rural social self-understandings on the other. These two, of course, inform one another—plenty of nonrural narratives have made their way into rural self-understandings, and plenty of rural self-understandings have found avenues into nonrural perceptions—and this interplay makes the task of sketching rural aesthetics also one of disambiguation. The chapter then moves to a discussion of rural solidarity, especially as seen through the lens of Flores's concept of aesthetic solidarity, and the chapter winds down with an examination of the nexus points between social structures, aesthetics, solidarity, and symbolization.

Aesthetic Solidarity: A Framework for Approaching Theological Aesthetics

A word may be warranted about why solidarity is an appropriate concept through which to view rural aesthetics. Briefly, aesthetics runs far deeper than what a particular community might find pretty or alluring. Aesthetic experience carries with it significant ethical content and implications, regardless of whether that content or those implications find explicit acknowledgment. As such, the work of ethics, in this case theological ethics, is integral to making sense of aesthetics and aesthetic experience. Additionally, aesthetic experiences can be prophetic or teleological, in that they can open imaginative possibilities for future life and orient current living toward them. In both cases—making sense of aesthetic experience and being inspired to live in certain ways by them—social life is implicated. This is no less the case in rural contexts;

2. Parts of this chapter are based on a research paper I presented at the 2024 meeting of the Catholic Theological Society of America (Benjamin Durheim, "Country Heaven: Toward a Rural Aesthetic of Salvation," paper presented at the 78th Annual Convention of the Catholic Theological Society of America, Baltimore, MD, June 2024).

aesthetic sensibilities are formed communally, aesthetic experiences resonate contextually, and consequently it is the architecture of social ethics—concepts like solidarity and the common good—that find most solid footing in sketching a rural aesthetics.

Recent work in theological ethics has taken serious account of these relationships between aesthetics and social ethics. In her book *The Aesthetics of Solidarity: Our Lady of Guadalupe and American Democracy*, Flores crafts an account of what she calls aesthetic solidarity, focusing contextually on the impact a particular religious symbol and aesthetic experience can have on American social life.[3] While Flores's focus is specifically on Latine approaches to theological aesthetics, her contextual approach resonates deeply with the work of discerning the contours of an American rural aesthetics. Distinguishing it from intellectual and practical solidarity,[4] Flores defines aesthetic solidarity as "an imaginative and affective basis for relationships that are characterized by mutuality, equality, and participation necessary for fostering the common good."[5] Drawing especially from Alejandro García-Rivera,[6] Flores argues that aesthetic experiences or encounters comprise necessary imaginative formation in grounding the work of solidarity for service to the common good. The ways by which one or a community approaches beauty cannot but impact how their vision of flourishing takes on flesh and how their hopes are crafted and sustained in the concrete circumstances of life. That this interfaces with solidarity, and

3. Flores, *The Aesthetics of Solidarity*.

4. Flores draws significantly on the work of David Hollenbach to illuminate intellectual solidarity and Ada María Isasi-Díaz to illuminate practical solidarity, among others (Flores, *The Aesthetics of Solidarity*, 124–136). See also David Hollenbach, *The Common Good and Christian Ethics* (Cambridge University, 2002), and Ada María Isasi-Díaz, *La Lucha Continues: Mujerista Theology* (Orbis, 2004).

5. Flores, *The Aesthetics of Solidarity*, 141.

6. Flores, *The Aesthetics of Solidarity*, particularly 106–118. See also Alejandro García-Rivera, *The Community of the Beautiful: A Theological Aesthetics* (Liturgical Press, 1999), or Alejandro García-Rivera, *A Wounded Innocence: Sketches for a Theology of Art* (Liturgical Press, 2003).

ultimately the common good, for Flores consists in how aesthetic experience operates affectively, in her words, "by cultivating affection for the good."[7] For the purposes of our current discussion, Flores's framework of aesthetic solidarity provides a way by which to engage some common affective sensibilities of rural Christian communities. What rural Christian communities experience as beautiful helps lay the foundation for rural conceptions of the common good and, ultimately, for many rural experiences of Christianity, a vision of the good life shared with God and each other toward which it is ordered.

There is another reason Flores's framework of aesthetic solidarity is helpful for conceptualizing a rural aesthetics: Flores takes great care to distinguish aesthetic approaches that order themselves toward solidarity and justice from those that order themselves away from solidarity and justice. In aesthetic experience, common bonds can germinate as easily for ill as for good. Flores cites the Unite the Right rally in Charlottesville, Virginia, in 2017 as a stark example of a malformed aesthetic experience, where "shared aesthetic symbols of Nazi salutes, the haze of tiki torches, and the vibrations of hate chants echoing across The Lawn at the University of Virginia" crafted a shared solidary experience, but it was one "untethered from adequate norms of justice."[8] In a word, not everything that a group finds attractive is therefore also—in the strict sense—beautiful. Rather, aesthetic experience needs always to be subject to ethical evaluation, or it loses its grounding. In this light, Flores names three "integral components"[9] in understanding aesthetic solidarity.

First, for Flores, aesthetic solidarity "concerns the formation of a community through aesthetic engagement or encounter with a medium in a way that its perceptible form is crucial to the formation of imagination and affections."[10] The *stuff* of aesthetic experience is not acci-

7. Flores, *The Aesthetics of Solidarity*, 130.

8. Flores, *The Aesthetics of Solidarity*, 11.

9. Flores, *The Aesthetics of Solidarity*, 141.

10. Flores, *The Aesthetics of Solidarity*, 141.

dental; it is essential for the experience to be what it is. As such, aesthetic experience is difficult or impossible to distill discursively, where it may be separated from encounter with the medium itself. Such binding of aesthetics to encounter does not preclude reflection on or theologizing about the encounter of course, but it does provide a helpful guard against eisegeting meaning or interpretation that decontextualizes the aesthetic experience. For example, the aesthetic experience of our exchange student guest as we drove through the December rural North Dakota snowstorm could not have been what it was *except by* mediation of the snowstorm, the driving, and the experience of that rural space. My description of that experience is not aesthetically equivalent to the experience itself. In a certain way, this may appear self-evident; few people would argue that descriptions of an experience capture the full meaning of going through the experience oneself. However, when the conversation turns from aesthetic experience to ethical interrogation and discernment of that experience, the necessary language mediation of such discernment can easily tempt a person to let go of or minimize the experiential and conceptual space between their understanding of an aesthetic experience, on the one hand, and the primary experience itself on the other. Judgmentalism does not always take note of the significant space between description of an experience and actually experiencing it.

Put differently, Chauvet's understanding of the presence of the absence is operative in aesthetics just as it is in liturgical/sacramental theology. In using language or expression to mediate an aesthetic experience to someone who has not personally undergone the experience but is trying to engage or evaluate it, the presence of that experience is conditioned by its very absence. The person to whom it is described is *removed* from the experience itself, which among other things shifts the "perceptible form" of the experience from whatever the original form was to description instead. This difference in form precipitates a presence of an absence, the truth of which in Chauvet's conception requires a kind of consent.[11] To avoid crafting a fiction of the aesthetic

11. Chauvet, *Symbol and Sacrament*, 177–178.

experience—an idol made in the image of one's own perspectives and biases—one needs to acknowledge and accept the real social space between oneself as conversation partner and the aesthetic experience that is the subject of conversation.

Beyond acknowledging the space between aesthetic experience and descriptions of it, Flores's first characteristic of aesthetic solidarity also, and perhaps primarily, emphasizes that changing the form of aesthetic experience ultimately changes the whole of the experience itself. If one takes a stroll through a rural woodland and experiences the natural beauty there but then tries to replicate the experience by attending a gallery of beautiful paintings of woodlands, the experience may rhyme, but it is not the same aesthetic experience. Even changing location is often sufficient to shift the aesthetic experience considerably—the cedar, spruce, and fir conifer forests running along the north shores of Lake Superior in Minnesota have an aesthetic that is strikingly different from the oak savannas that run south through the Midwest. One might object that a stroll through the forest is a stroll through the forest—the form of the aesthetic experience has not changed—but that is part of the point; those living within an operative aesthetic framework may experience differences in form, where others simply see distinctions between content. However, if the aesthetic experience is inseparable from the form it takes, the reality of the experience hinges not first on external evaluation but on the experience of those who have taken it as *formative*.

Second for Flores, "the community united through aesthetic experience ought to be characterized by relationships of mutuality, equality, and participation that foster human dignity."[12] By this I do not read Flores to mean that the community needs to be ethically flawless in order to read aesthetic solidarity as operative there; instead, to the degree that aesthetic experience plays a formative part in cultivating community, it needs to embody these aspects (mutuality, equality, participation) that are ordered toward human dignity. Every community will have its shortcomings and failings. The question is whether the

12. Flores, *The Aesthetics of Solidarity*, 141.

shared, formative aesthetic experiences of that community exacerbate or resist those shortcomings.

Often enough shared aesthetic experiences will include aspects that are both socially healthy and those that are not. Take for example the fireworks displays that many small towns in America put on in celebration either of Independence Day or of a local town festival and sometimes both. For many in the community, these may mediate experiences of bonding and togetherness with friends, family, and neighbors as they gather just after dark on a summer evening to witness the sky light up with exploding lights and sparkles. For others, in particular those for whom such explosions evoke past experiences of armed conflict or trauma, the displays may mediate a community's disregard for their mental health or peace. For others still, community fireworks displays can mediate a kind of adjacent excuse to put on private pyrotechnic shows, which can easily mix with a kind of "I can do whatever I want on my own property" mentality, exacerbated in places where such private fireworks shows are illegal. This multivalence of aesthetic experience invites social-ethical discernment because these distinct experiences may overlap or even cohere together in particular persons and communities. Social life is often messy, which means that aesthetic solidarity—if it is to be solidary at all—needs to form a community toward rather than away from human dignity.

Third and finally, the community engaged in aesthetic solidarity must "seek a fostering of justice as the minimal level of solidarity required for human flourishing and the common good."[13] To fail in this regard—to seek something less than justice as an acceptable form of solidarity in service to the common good—would be to undermine aesthetic solidarity by diluting it. This may appear obvious, but it can be a frustratingly common temptation to substitute something like "progress" or "baby steps in the right direction" for justice. Simply because an aesthetic encounter or set of experiences helps a community imagine and move toward relationships or systems that "aren't as bad as they used to be" doesn't mean it has therefore participated in aesthetic solidarity.

13. Flores, *The Aesthetics of Solidarity*, 141.

This third aspect of aesthetic solidarity can be a sticking point in the relationship between the rural and the nonrural. As Wuthnow has pointed out, it is exactly in conceptions of justice, morality, and values that rural contexts tend to harbor a deep suspicion of nonrural ones, and nonrural contexts seem to want to correct or fix rural ones.[14] The partisan and voting disparities between rural and nonrural areas of the United States are just one symptom that is emblematic of differing approaches to and understandings of justice.[15] However, it would be a mistake to conclude therefore that rural America has a cohesive and monolithic understanding of justice that is in competition with the nonrural. Understandings of justice are also formed aesthetically, just as aesthetic experiences may be ordered toward or away from justice. This means that part of the work of understanding rural social ethics is understanding the diverse and sometimes discordant aesthetic sensibilities that give shape to rural perspectives. The goal cannot be simply to reduce rural aesthetics to either ethical bankruptcy or ethical perfection. Rather, to make sense of rural social reality and the social ethics operative there, aesthetic experience—mediated through the process of symbolization—is an indispensable formative part. Rural aesthetics is neither wholly innocent nor wholly malevolent; it merits evaluation on the basis of aesthetic solidarity from both the perspectives of justice operative within it and for those who are drawn to and/or formed by a rural aesthetic.

Within this framework of aesthetic solidarity, the discussion can now move to asking in what ways and to what degree rural communities—especially understood as rural communities in which Christianity has a significant cultural footprint—exhibit aesthetic sensibilities that cohere as a rural aesthetic capable of aesthetic solidarity.

---

14. See Wuthnow, *The Left Behind*, esp. chaps. 4 and 5.

15. Though this is hardly reducible only to a rural versus nonrural problem. For a discussion of how states that tend to the political right understand "justice" in relation to politics, see Robert Wuthnow, *Red State Religion: Faith and Politics in America's Heartland* (Princeton University, 2012).

Sketching a Rural Aesthetic

An exhaustive account of rural aesthetic sensibilities would not be feasible here; the diversity of rural spaces and perspectives in the United States is vast enough to prohibit such a claim. However, there are certain overarching commonalities of aesthetics that run through many rural areas, and these deserve some attention, not unlike the narratives from chapter 1. As a springboard for much of this part of the discussion, I use the research that I and my student collaborators conducted in rural Christian liturgical communities, not because Christianity has a monopoly on rural aesthetics but because our research suggested a close tie between Christian ritual practice and wider rural aesthetic sensibilities that are given symbolic voice therein. Christian liturgy is symbol-rich as a practice, but its symbolization diffuses beyond the rituals themselves when the operative liturgical aesthetics resonate with the wider contextual aesthetic sensibilities in which liturgy is embedded. Reading the aesthetics of rural Christian ritual yields a privileged view into the aesthetics that hold sway in rural American contexts more generally.

"I always feel better after a church service." This statement, made by an elderly woman we interviewed in response to a question about why she attends the particular rural church she does, encapsulates the underlying tone of many of the rural Christians we spoke with. The questions we brought to our interviews in 2022 and 2023 focused on hope, anger, frustration, and experiences of religious and social power structures. Again and again, interviewees grounded their responses in liturgical experiences, usually Sunday morning mass or church services. The overarching sense seemed to be that it really mattered what liturgy made affectively real—the aesthetics of liturgy mattered. A few interviewees spoke of liturgical or doctrinal content (the importance of "knowing the Bible," the relevance of preaching on contemporary issues, etc.), but nearly without fail each interviewee spoke in some regard to aesthetic experiences of liturgy. By this I don't simply mean liturgical artifacts that most obviously interface with aesthetics such as music, architecture, procession, or movement; I mean liturgical experiences that spoke to our interviewees *in an aesthetic key*. For example, the presence or absence of certain bodies like local-resident bodies, commuters, or children conditioned the aesthetics of liturgy as much as or more than which hymns were sung. The recapitulation of familiar, even localized values in fellowship and preaching spoke in an aesthetic language more readily accessed than that of the rites and rubrics. Often enough even just the occurrence of liturgy itself in a particular church building made real much more than the local architecture; it conditioned congregants' aesthetic experience, given voice in emotion, of the relationships between that church and its local community, as well as its wider ecclesial communion. These aesthetic sensibilities could be categorized in many different ways, but I'd like to name three that happen also to largely resonate with wider sociological findings in studies of rural American social reality: local stability, independence tempered by local authority, and neighborliness.

By *local stability*, I mean the sense that there perseveres a longstanding, resilient local character or identity to which a person or group belongs. Put negatively, *in*stability is a near-constant danger for many rural communities. Wuthnow points out that natural and human-made disasters, even more than out-migration or loss of jobs, have proven a potent threat to rural community vitality.[16] Simply in terms of the logistics of crafting a shared social life, disasters can test the resilience of small communities in ways from which they may never recover—grocery stores may not return, financial relief or aid may be slow to arrive or may not arrive at all, homes may not be rebuilt if families flee and do not return, and a host of other emergent circumstances may curtail the life of a small community in ways that a larger community may be able to more easily weather simply by virtue of their population. Beyond these nuts-and-bolts considerations, rural consciousness (in Cramer's terms) writes into many rural narratives the sense that the rural way of life is under threat. If rural consciousness is characterized by feeling ignored by centers of power and not given a fair share of resources, among other

16. Wuthnow, *The Left Behind*, 46–47.

characteristics, then it becomes relatively straightforward to read many rural difficulties—the difficulty of sustaining family farms, declining population, school or church closings, loss of local businesses, lack of access to health care and eldercare, among a host of other issues—as reflections of a way of life under siege.

Positively, then, against this narrative backdrop of rural precariousness, local stability is a beautiful thing, an integral part of making the rural life the rural *good* life. When our interviewees spoke of their church experiences in rural communities, many of them spoke approvingly of the long relationships that their church community had had with the wider small town, often going back generations prior to their own membership. The perseverance of the local liturgical community symbolized—mediated the social reality of—a local stability that could be read through the community's history, constituting an aesthetic contour of the community's social life. The forms of this aesthetic experience vary far beyond Christian liturgical experience, but very often when this aesthetic sensibility found voice, its symbolization was tied to a particular church building as much as any sense of a liturgical community or assembly. Such a connection is likely familiar to anyone with experience in rural Christian ministry; often rural church finances are tight, and ecclesial centers of power take on the unwelcome burden of figuring out how to staff—or outright close—churches whose membership cannot support full-time pastoral ministry. This was a problem in some of the communities we engaged, and while no interviewee denied the difficulty of keeping particular rural church buildings open, when the subject of combining or closing churches came up, more than pragmatism was at stake. To close a church was also received in an aesthetic key, an offense against local stability mediated by the operation of the church building. The actions of consolidating or closing church communities have a significant symbolic depth.

Local stability also moves beyond the strictly social. For many, rural aesthetics related to local stability includes the stability of local expressions of the natural world. This may be most obvious in agrarian rural contexts, where the cadence of the seasons dictates much of social and economic life. Maintaining a healthy, stable relationship with the land that one works is part of making a good life on that land,[17] though of course perspectives vary widely regarding exactly what a stable relationship with the land entails; a large conventional industrial agricultural practice may have a significantly different understanding than a small organic farm, for example. Beyond agriculture, however, pastimes that engage the natural world (fishing, hunting, hiking, camping, etc.) often thrive in rural contexts, weaving their way into the fabric of a rural aesthetic.

Stability can be ordered toward justice and human dignity, but taking Flores's framework seriously, it is also worthwhile to note that it can be twisted away from these as well. For example, the length of time it takes for a rural community to adopt a newcomer as a local, as a part of *this* community's stability, can depend on several factors, sometimes including race, ethnicity, linguistic tradition, and other identity markers. Racism and xenophobia can embed themselves behind the mask of local pride and concern, transmuting local stability from an aspect of aesthetic solidarity into individual and social sin. If liturgy can embody local stability as part of a healthy rural aesthetic, it must take care to disentangle local belonging from localized supremacy, often mingled with racism.

Moving to the second marker of a rural aesthetic that emerged, independence can sometimes be mistaken for individualism, and I want to take care not to do that here. When I name independence tempered by local authority as a rural aesthetic sensibility, I mean that our interviewees largely exhibited a sense that the common good primarily refers to the local community (church or social) and then *consequently*—even subsequently—refers to wider human communities.[18] Subsidiarity was

17. This, of course, carries theological ramifications as well. See, for example, Micah D. Kiel, *Apocalyptic Ecology: The Book of Revelation, Earth, and the Future* (Liturgical Press, 2017).

18. In early 2025, some echoes of this made it into the center of the public eye when Vice President JD Vance seemed to identify this tendency with the *ordo amoris*, claiming "You love your family, and then you love your neighbor, and then you love

alive and well in this, with interviewees regularly connecting hope to responsibility for particular relationships in their local community. For example, one interviewee who is a member of what many would call a thriving rural liturgical community lamented that the local municipal community (whose population is roughly two hundred) was underrepresented in the church's life. Many church participants commuted in from significant distances, leading this interviewee to wonder in what sense the local community is responsible for the church and vice versa. This the interviewee cast in a tone of valuing independence as a guard against the church being swept up in nonlocal social concerns and conflicts. Independence in this sense was not about the individual interviewee's concern but about how the small community can practice

---

your community, and then you love your fellow citizens in your own country. And then after that, you can focus and prioritize the rest of the world" (JD Vance, qtd. in Associated Press, "What Is 'Ordo Amoris?' Vice President JD Vance Invokes This Medieval Catholic Concept," Associated Press, February 6, 2025, https://apnews.com/article/jd-vance-catholic-theology-migration-e868af574fb2e742c6ed3d756c569769). A flurry of public theological debate ensued, some defending Vance's view and many theological authorities, including Pope Francis, critiquing the view (see, for example, Allison Prang, "JD Vance 'Surprised' by Pushback from Pope, US Bishops on Immigration," *National Catholic Reporter*, February 28, 2025, https://www.ncronline.org/news/vance-surprised-pushback-pope-us-bishops-new-immigration-policies, or Stephen J. Pope, "The Problem with JD Vance's Theology of 'Ordo Amoris'—And Its Impact on Policy," *America*, February 13, 2025, https://www.americamagazine.org/faith/2025/02/13/ordo-amoris-stephen-pope-vance-249926, or James Orr, "JD Vance States the Obvious About *Ordo Amoris*," *First Things*, January 31, 2025, https://firstthings.com/jd-vance-states-the-obvious-about-ordo-amoris/). My point here is not to engage deeply Vance's unfortunate perspective on the ordering of loves; it is to draw a distinction between his politically-popularized approach and the one that seemed on display in our interviews with rural Christians (to which we also return later in this text). While Vance appears to hold the perspective that the ordering of loves is an order of priority, the rural perspectives we engaged appeared to focus on locality as a result of their conviction that loving one's neighbor is a fundamental Christian tenet, and the physically proximate neighbor is the one to which they have most immediate access for embodied actions of love and solidarity. This does not mean prioritizing the local over and against distant neighbors; from a rural perspective, it is through loving the persons who are physically close and depend on you that the universal love of neighbor flows. These are not competitive loves; they are mutually informing and enriching.

responsibility for itself and where the centers of the church's authority resided. The aesthetic sensibility in this and similar remarks in other interviews appeared to be that it is a beautiful thing to be able to rely on the local, where community members are known by name and relationship—a close and sometimes even intimate knowledge that begets local responsibility not as a task but as a gift.

Often enough, independence tempered by local authority can be mediated vocationally. Wuthnow notes this in his studies of American farmers, who largely include independence and self-reliance as positive aspects of their economic enterprises.[19] This can be a problem, however, as the very concept of the "independent farmer" has been significantly eroded by everything from greatly diminished choices regarding what to plant or raise, to decreased ownership and oversight of the tools and machinery they use, to reliance on the fluctuations of global marketplaces. Similar stories could be read outside of agriculture, but the aesthetic ideal of independence that is conversant with *local* rather than external authority remains a significant piece of rural aesthetics. Sometimes rarity is a part of what conditions aesthetic sensibility, and in those places where rural independence flourishes, often so, too, does a strong sense of pride and satisfaction in the fact that it does so.

Third, neighborliness roughly means an embedded sense that it matters to practice care for those whose lives unfold close to yours. This may sound quite close to many understandings of solidarity, and perhaps it is, but a central characterizing aspect of rural neighborliness is that, when done well, it is largely immune to the destructive tendencies of division, whether political, religious, or otherwise. To live physically close to someone is to participate in their flourishing (or lack thereof) and to have that participation reciprocated. Sometimes interviewees spoke of this in terms of acts of service (providing transportation, childcare, meals, etc. for neighbors who needed them), but oftentimes interviewees spoke in liturgical terms, citing prayers and church liturgical structures that acted as part conversation with -God, part community

19. See Wuthnow, *In the Blood*, esp. chap. 4.

information, and part call to prayer and action. The liturgical community operated as a social center in the conception of many interviewees, and they experienced this as beautiful. As one interviewee quipped in relation to her diagnosis of breast cancer, "I haven't put that in the bulletin yet, but it will go on next week, and I'm asking for the prayers in my church." Subsumed in this statement was an aesthetic sense that it was beautiful not simply to be prayed for but to be prayed for by a community of people whose names she knew, with whom she has relationships, who are her neighbors.

Neighborliness is not a magic bullet to fix divisions, but the affective sense of neighborliness is a strong aspect that emerged out of both my research and the rural immersion programs I facilitate. More than once during immersion programming, participants have pressed our immersion partners regarding why they do things the way they do when it is clear to everyone involved that there may be financial incentive to do otherwise. In most of these exchanges, our partners—from farmers to bankers to ministers—cite a strong sense that what it means to be part of their local community includes doing what is most beneficial for their community and the people in it, not simply what is most financially expedient for themselves. These exchanges have included stories of hardship and long hours of uncompensated work, told with a kind of affective satisfaction that they resulted in real benefits for neighbors in the community. Service beyond self-interest is, in many rural communities, a category of action that mediates neighborliness. It carries and helps write the symbolic depth of the community; it is a kind of symbolizing action.

Like local stability, both independence tempered by local authority and neighborliness are susceptible to twistings of social sin. If a community isolates itself, or if one begins to decide which neighbors "count" as neighbors and which can be dispensed with, the aesthetic sensibilities can turn away from solidarity and toward sin. Good liturgical practice can be a guard against that, and this is honestly the space to which these summers of research led. The fact that so many interviewees spoke about liturgical experience in relation to their understandings of hope and the common good points to a significant role that Christian worship practice plays in forming a rural aesthetic of hope and salvation that is solidary rather than sinful. In many of the rural Christian communities we engaged, this seems already to be taking place in worship and liturgical practice. Such formation opens questions of why this is not more widespread in rural Christianity and why counterexamples of rural aesthetics—sometimes liturgically informed—that are twisted to amoral or cynical political aims can sometimes loom so large in conceptions of the rural. That question draws more attention in chapters 5 and 6, but prior to that, it is worthwhile to move toward examining the relationship between rural aesthetics and rural solidarity.

Rural Solidarity

Drawing from Flores's framework of aesthetic solidarity, it is necessary to account for whether and in what ways rural aesthetics interfaces with expressions of solidarity that fulfill the second and third markers of aesthetic solidarity, namely that the aesthetics should be ordered toward supporting human dignity and that justice is a *sine qua non* requirement for solidarity. Assessing these two markers invites a return to contextual rural self-understanding because the ways that justice and human dignity take on concrete flesh are mediated by the social and individual bodies in which they find expression. This is, of course, *not* to say that there are no universal norms of justice or of human dignity (far from it); rather, mediating justice and human dignity into social reality requires an attention to and engagement with the relevant social context. For example, when many folks hear the word *justice*, they may (rightly) think of its classic definition of rendering to each person what is due. That definition of justice has a long and storied history, and it works well so far as it goes. However, theological ethicists such as Margaret Farley have moved their understandings of justice further, not supplanting the classic definition but enriching it with attentiveness to contextual realities. As Farley explains, justice should include the principle that "persons and groups of persons ought to be affirmed according to their concrete reality, actual and potential."[20] Discernment of social reality is integral to discernment of justice.

This is simply to say that understanding solidarity in a rural key requires more than just importing some generic concept of solidarity into rural spaces. Rural solidarity is only *rural* by mediation of rural social reality, which includes the influential narrative of rural communities as moral communities. Recall that Wuthnow's explanation of rural moral community centers on the affective senses of feeling at home and "doing the right things"—both affections that can be read as part of the rural aesthetic sense of local stability—conditioned not only by these feelings themselves but additionally by the localized mediation of these affections.[21] In this sense, the moral community also participates in symbolization; to be a part of *this* or *that* rural moral community mediates meaning and identity in a deeper and more specific way than if one were to identify with being part of *a* moral community in general. Rural social identity is often inseparable from the symbolizing mediation of a particular moral community.

Solidarity then, in a rural key, has as its primary referent the relationships between physically proximate neighbors who mutually recognize their belonging in and to the local moral community. As such, the aesthetics tied to and evocative of rural solidarity includes things like local stability, independence tempered by local authority, and neighborliness. Solidarity itself is not *simply* affective, however; it is, in the words of M. Shawn Copeland, "a set of body-practices."[22] Copeland points out that the term *solidarity* is relatively new to theological discourse, but the reality it connotes, "the empathetic incarnation of Christian love,"[23] is

---

20. Margaret Farley, *Just Love: A Framework for Christian Sexual Ethics* (Continuum, 2006), 208–209.

21. See Wuthnow, *The Left Behind*, esp. chap. 1.

22. Copeland, *Enfleshing Freedom*, 2. For a discussion of theological aesthetics in relation to bodily vulnerability, see Susie Paulik Babka, *Through the Dark Field: The Incarnation Through an Aesthetics of Vulnerability* (Liturgical Press, 2017).

23. Copeland, *Enfleshing Freedom*, 93.

as old as Christianity itself and is mediated by actions of standing with those experiencing hardship, oppression, violence, or tragedy. In this way, solidarity is much more than simply kindness or civility—a point that Flores also makes.[24] Solidarity is the practice of "service to and for others and for the kingdom of God."[25]

In many rural contexts, solidarity is mediated by belonging to the local moral community. Hardship can be a close neighbor in rural contexts, and the moral community itself is conditioned by the idea that weathering hardship is rarely something one does alone. Instead, body practices of neighbors and the community as a whole can ease hardship or exacerbate it, and when rural solidarity is practiced well, the practices themselves can undergo symbolization, mediating the presence not simply of the primary practitioners but also of the whole moral community. Often enough, these practices that include symbolic depth are relatively everyday activities, repeated and shared until they become an accepted norm in a moral community, the "right things" that one does not because one is conscious of how good one is acting but simply because it is part of one's social identity to do so.

Supporting local businesses can be illuminative of this kind of everyday practice of rural solidarity. The survival of a locally owned and operated small-town or rural business evokes all three major aspects of rural aesthetics: It contributes to services and job availability that buttress stability, it resists the exportation of oversight and accountability, and it directly impacts the financial well-being of one's neighbors. In addition, the survival of local businesses bears directly on the social identities of those who are part of the rural moral community. For example, there is a delightful flower shop in the small town neighboring my own, a second-generation business owned by a set of siblings. Their prices are competitive, though not the cheapest, and their attention to detail and interaction with clients tend to take priority over speed of service. My children love going there because they know that it'll usually take about

24. Flores, *The Aesthetics of Solidarity*, 126–129.

25. Copeland, *Enfleshing Freedom*, 93.

thirty minutes or more from the time we walk in to when we walk out with a bouquet, during which time I'll chat with the owner-operators, and the kids get to play with the attention-loving and affectionate cats who make their home at the shop. Flowers are a luxury, but when we visit the flower shop, we are not *simply* buying flowers. We are participating in an accepted local practice of social solidarity that long predates us; we are playing a small part in building what it means to be small-town neighbors.

The primary character of the local in the exercise of rural solidarity can also be a contentious point, however. The flower shop is a relatively benign example because in it, the action of solidarity does not encounter significant competition with other actions that could also be solidary. Another example may illustrate this: When I was growing up, my paternal grandparents, who live in rural west-central Minnesota, had a neighbor who was known to hunt deer year-round. This was not legal, as deer hunting was and is fairly tightly regulated in Minnesota and takes place in autumn, with particular regulations applying to local places for hunting, particular methods of hunting, and so on.[26] Of course, the object of those regulations is (at their best) to ensure the health of Minnesota's collective deer herd and thereby to support the common good in relation both to natural resources and human interaction with them. Respecting these regulations can be a solidary action; poaching is not. However, one year when I asked my father about the year-round hunting habits of the neighbor, he explained firmly that the neighbor was a person of very limited financial means, and venison was a meat supply—sometimes the only meat supply—that he could access.

This was far from a glib dismissal of environmental regulation—my father was and remains deeply dedicated to responsibly maintaining the health of the natural world we inhabit. It was, as I interpreted it, a conviction that a neighbor's hunger made a stronger ethical demand than that neighbor's accountability to Department of Natural Resources regulations. This conviction appeared to be shared by most or all the other close rural community members; I never heard of a report or penalty

26. See Minnesota Department of Natural Resources, "Deer Hunting," accessed March 18, 2025, https://www.dnr.state.mn.us/hunting/deer/index.html.

taking place in the case of this neighbor. My point is not to prescribe an ethical judgment of the situation; the point is that rural aesthetic solidarity mediated local authority and neighborliness as primary operative sensibilities rather than the less-localized regulations of the Minnesota DNR. Poaching is still a detestable thing in this context, but as the community members saw it, this neighbor's practice was something other than poaching; it invited solidarity, not accusation.

Taken together, rural aesthetic solidarity is legible from a rural perspective. The primary aspects of rural aesthetics (local stability, independence tempered by local authority, and neighborliness) translate into a solidarity that prioritizes the well-being of local persons and the local community. Justice, in this sense, is contextualized, and human dignity is an ideal made sensible in the individual and social bodies that make up the rural moral community. This process of "making sensible" is also one of symbolization; practices of aesthetic solidarity include symbolic depth that mediates *more* than just aesthetic solidarity. When a school survives, the town has more than just access to education; it has a formative social center. When a church survives, the local context has more than a place of worship; it has (ideally) an embodied, visible social dedication to the practices of loving God and neighbor. When a business survives, the community has more than just access to particular goods and services; it has a richer social life and identity. When a person survives and staves off hunger, more than just that person's body survives; the integrity of the moral community survives. None of this is automatic or assured; it takes action and dedication on the part of the constituent elements of a rural moral community. In a word, it takes aesthetic solidarity. That does not mean, however, that such action is not structurally conditioned. It is to the interplay of rural structures, symbolization, and aesthetics that this discussion now turns by way of conclusion.

Conclusion: Aesthetics, Structure, and Symbol

Just as it is essential in liturgical/sacramental theology to acknowledge the space between raw sensation and full perception, or between reality itself and our understanding of that reality (Chauvet's presence of the absence), it is important to emphasize that the connection between aesthetics and the concrete actions of aesthetic solidarity is a *mediated* connection, not an *im*mediate one. Practices of aesthetic solidarity necessarily take place in social contexts, which bear the developmental marks of the morphogenetic cycle and processes of symbolization. Social interactions are mediated in part by the structural conditioning that precedes them, as well as by the symbolic order that operates in a given context to which aesthetics contributes. A truth not unique to rural contexts is that one can find something beautiful, compelling, desirable, or worthy and be structurally inhibited from pursuing it. Likewise, social structures can also form contexts within which it is easier or more straightforward to pursue life according to the socially formed aesthetic sensibilities that one has. In both cases, there is a space between aesthetic sensibility and concrete action that is mediated by the structural conditioning of a social context.

This structural conditioning, informed also by the protostructural gesturing of the process of symbolization, is an integral part of how social interactions like aesthetic solidarity take on flesh. It would be incorrect to intuit that a social sense of aesthetics translates immediately into social action ordered toward resonance with that sense of aesthetics; between aesthetic sensibilities and social action there is a process mediated through structure and symbolization. Unfortunately, however, it is not an altogether uncommon mistake to interpret aesthetics in the reverse: If a person or a community acts in a certain way, so the thinking goes, that must reveal something about the aesthetic sensibilities and values of that person or community. In a certain way, this may appear logical—actions speak louder than words—but to reduce rural aesthetics or values to the data of externally interpreted actions is to miss both the depth of symbolism and the impact of social structure.

An example may help: In the growing season of 2024, the farmer who has rented much of the farmland around my retired paternal grandparents' home applied for, and was accepted as part of, a pilot program for a new method of fertilizing and tilling the fields. While it required specific equipment, the new method would reduce the amount of fertilizer used and combine certain steps of the fieldwork process so he could eliminate one or even two equipment passes over each field, significantly cutting down on the labor, time, and other inputs each field required to be brought to harvest. This made both financial and logistical sense, with the added bonus of being good for the soil itself and the surrounding environment; it was altogether good news. Unfortunately, his work with the new equipment early in the season ran into considerable technical difficulties, which required weeks of troubleshooting and repair by technicians from the pilot program before he could undertake the work of planting his crops. Then, as sometimes happens in lines of work that are dictated by the weather, his work was further delayed by more than an additional two weeks because of the near-nonstop rainfall that washed through central Minnesota at that time.

By this point, May 31 had come and gone, without his being able to get the crop seeds in the ground. This is a significant deadline because if his crops were not planted before May 31, anything he *would* plant in the fields thereafter would be ineligible for crop insurance. The growing season is not generally long enough to support insuring crops that are planted after May 31; the danger of losses due to frost, snow, and other factors prior to harvest becomes too high. At this point, then, he had a choice: He could either (1) plant the crops anyway and gamble that they would yield a harvest before weather prevented them from doing so (thereby risking wholescale loss of his inputs on those fields) or (2) exercise the prevented-planting clause in his crop insurance, which would not only cover the costs associated with keeping the fields but also requires that no salable crop be planted on those fields in the current year (to prevent exploitation of the clause by claiming prevented planting and then sowing and harvesting a crop anyway).

From his perspective, the choice was unpleasant but clear: The safest bet would be to exercise the prevented-planting clause and leave the fields fallow for the 2024 season. He didn't like it, but he had to do it as part of sustaining stability in his overall farming enterprise. That isn't the point; lots of vocations require unpleasant and difficult choices.

The point is how the choice impacted my grandparents, whose reaction I share with their permission. Their back porch overlooks two of the largest fields on the property, and a significant amount of their aesthetic experience of the farm, baked in by fifty years of working the land, is tied to the productivity of the farm. Witnessing the crops grow through the year is more than observation for them; the symbolism of the fields and what they grow runs deep. The crops mediate more than simply production and economic endeavor; they mediate *home* and *vocation*. Gazing out over bare fields that have not lain fallow in nearly fifty-five years, they shared, mediated an affective experience—call it sadness, melancholy, or something similar—that was inescapable. The fallow fields arrested their aesthetic sensibilities, mediating a particular kind of sorrowful meaning to them.

My point in relating this story is not to romanticize or overdramatize it. The choice to exercise the prevented-planting clause was not a point of contention between my grandparents and the farmer; all parties involved knew that this was an all but necessary step, and no resentment or strife soured the relationship as a result. That said, the aesthetics didn't fit. The overlapping effects of structures like the crop insurance, the pilot fertilization/tilling program, and renting the fields themselves precipitated action *against* the shared aesthetic sensibilities of both the farmer and my grandparents, with affective results. Additionally, this is one individual story. Consider in years of environmental hardship (drought, flood, etc.) the social effects of entire communities living into this kind of aesthetic dissonance, or the experiences of nonagrarian rural communities weathering other kinds of structural challenges, and it should be clear that attention to aesthetic sensibilities and the symbolizations that mediate them are more than mere add-ons to social reality. They are primary ways that social reality is mediated into social perception. In the case of my grandparents in 2024, the action of leaving the fields fallow gestured toward a protostructure of the farm conceived as *not* necessarily a crop-producing social unit (something aesthetically untenable for them), which flowed into the shared morphogenetic helix of their rural moral community. It is not that the social context changed dramatically; it is that understanding the social context necessarily includes a literacy regarding the depth of symbolization in acts like these. Without that, even actions that are born of the best intentions and undertaken with the greatest care can beget social misfires or distress.

Thus far, our discussion has largely engaged symbolizations in which the best of intentions and good faith are operative. In an effort to lay out and clarify the relationships among symbol, social ethics, and social change in rural American contexts, we have put off engaging those processes of symbolization in which malevolence and social sin *are* clearly operative. However, social sin is operative in rural places just as it is operative in nonrural ones, and it is to those twistings of social reality—when symbolization mediates evil and strife rather than solidarity and the common good—that we must now turn.

CHAPTER FIVE

Symbolization and Sin in Rural America

Introduction: Sin and Symbols

CAN SYMBOLS SIN? I begin with this question *not* because I think they can. Indeed, an immediate, knee-jerk set of responses may be that of course they can't; symbols are not agents, they do not have free will, they do not take actions on their own, and they are not centers of consciousness capable of knowing right from wrong. None of these responses is incorrect, but they all function within a framework for understanding sin itself that suggests sin is reducible to the actions taken by an agent with some amount of freedom to discern and follow through on those actions. In a word, they fall into one side of "the vexatious fact of society"—that of individualism—that Archer and critical realist sociology work to resolve.[1] Likewise, it is unhelpful to fall into the opposite side—collectivism—which may maintain that the likelihood of sin is deterministically laid out by the social circumstances within which individuals exist. Rather, having suggested in chapter 3 that symbolization participates in a kind of protostructural formation of social reality, chapter 5 now considers how symbols as protostructures interface with destructive ethical reality, with sin.

A word may be warranted here about what I mean by the term *sin*. It is a term woven into the fabric of theological inquiry, and it has taken many meanings and connotations throughout the discipline's history. For our purposes, the most helpful definition is the one articulated by James F. Keenan in his book *A History of Catholic Theological Ethics*: Sin

1. Archer, *Realist Social Theory*, 1–16.

is, in Keenan's words, "the failure to bother to love."[2] Sin is not simply the committing of an evil act or an offense against God; to avoid sin, one must love. Even this might mistakenly be read as an overly individualistic reduction of the concept of sin to particular actions by agents, but Keenan's understanding of sin does indicate an attention to the structural components of the concept.[3] To love—or to fail to do so—always takes place within particular historical and social circumstances that inform that love or its lack. To attend to symbol in relation to sin, then, requires asking whether, in what ways, and to what degree symbols and acts of symbolization inhibit or facilitate practices of love.

Asking this question of how symbols and their symbolization catalyze or inhibit practices of love is complex for a number of reasons. First, addressing the question requires an account of how social structures interface with sin and love; this is the subject of this chapter's first section. Since I have suggested that symbols and symbolization are not themselves social structures but rather operate in a manner of protostructural social gesturing or development between social action and structural elaboration, their impacts on and formation by practices of sin and love are not reducible only to structural analysis. The contributions of critical realist sociology and the theological ethicists who have engaged it get us only so far in reckoning with symbol and sin. Beyond that, ritual and practices of symbolization throw light on how symbol functions protostructurally, particularly through categories of causality linked to gift-giving and gratuitousness rather than instrumentalization.

Second, because symbols and symbolization are contextually bound, it is necessary to engage particular symbols and symbolizations in order to approach the symbolic orders within which they operate. Rural American contexts are no exception to this; mediation of meaning *is* contextual mediation of meaning, making contextual engagement essential for reception of symbolic mediation. The significant complicating factor in this, however, is that context is built by symbolization,

2. James F. Keenan, *A History of Catholic Theological Ethics* (Paulist, 2022), 22.

3. Keenan, *A History of Catholic Theological Ethics*, esp. chap. 8.

just as contextual literacy is required for engaging symbolization. It is a bit of a chicken-and-egg problem; to fully receive the mediation of symbolic meaning, one needs to be formed by the context within which that symbolization takes place, but such formation is also necessarily mediated by the symbolic. Additionally, this is as true for those within a context as for those witnessing the context from the outside. The diversity of contextual expressions of "rural" makes for a diversity of protostructural conditioning within rural contexts. This does not mean that there *is* no discernible context that can be called rural; it means that, just as in other social contexts, social reality is varied, complex, and multifaceted.

The second, third, and fourth sections of this chapter work to address this complexity. In doing so, it is important to note that it is not possible to exhaustively capture the fullness of how particular symbols interface with sin and love in rural contexts. Such has been part of the point of this book: Symbol operates in practice often more than in discourse, so discourse can only capture so much. Nevertheless, the second section of the chapter attends to symbolization as it has interfaced with the sins of racism and white supremacy in rural contexts. In doing so, my goal is to speak some amount of truth about harmful symbols that operate as inhibitors to practices of love; it is *not* my goal to suggest that rural contexts are somehow uniquely bigoted or hate-filled. As mentioned earlier in the discussion, racism, sexism, xenophobia, and other social sins find homes in nonrural spaces just as in rural ones. Their symbolization, however, is not easily transferable between rural and nonrural contexts.

The third and fourth sections of the chapter focus on what I am calling *symbolic reductionism* (the third section) and *lying symbols* (the fourth section). By *symbolic reductionism*, I mean the role of symbols and symbolization in dehumanizing persons by excluding essential components of their social realities in favor of overemphasizing only one or a few. Symbolic reductionism might be read as analogous to stereotyping, but there is more to it than overgeneralization or bias. Symbolic reductionism operates, for example, in single-issue politics, where the issue itself takes on symbolic weight and meaning, disordering conceptions of the common good in order to exclusively focus on itself rather than interfacing with the multifaceted social realities of which it is a part. Symbolic reductionism also works to create "others" and demonize them and to venerate local conceptions of common sense, falsely isolating a place from its wider social context. This leads into the fourth section's treatment of lying symbols, by which I mean symbolizations that mediate untruths into social realities. This can take the form of concocting fantasy worlds untethered from data and wider experience, caricaturing social realities to fit such fantasies, and/or mediations of disinformation in order to buttress them.

Running throughout this chapter is a constant central difficulty of symbol: the multivalence of symbolization. Symbolic mediation of meaning and social reality is contextually conditioned, but that does *not* mean that a symbol *only* mediates meaning within its home context. Symbols can and do speak far beyond the social realities that gave them birth, sometimes in languages that would be unrecognizable to their original contexts. Put differently, symbols mean different things to different people and communities, depending on how their familiarity with and formation into the relevant symbolic orders have taken place. This does not mean that symbolization is therefore reducible to subjectivism or relativism. Symbols do not speak whatever someone or a group wants them to. Symbols speak *many things at the same time*, and only some of those things are mediated to any particular person or entity who participates in or witnesses the symbolization, depending on their contextual formation. The same symbol may be read to help facilitate practices of love and solidarity from one contextual perspective and by that very facilitation be read to inhibit practices of love from other contextual perspectives. Symbolization is messy not just conceptually but also ethically.

Reading Sin and Symbol Structurally

A persistent problem in speaking of social or structural sin is the relationship between such sin and the agency of individual and communal entities that participate in it.[4] If one conceives of social structures in the ways critical realist sociology suggests—that they are sets of relationships between entities in a social context—it can be difficult to assign agency to the relationship/structure itself. Instead, agency belongs to the persons or communal entities enmeshed in the structure(s), but as critical realist sociology insists, that agency is conditioned by the structures themselves. The structures of a social context reward certain exercises of individual and communal agency and punish others. They enable and facilitate consideration of some options for action while also inhibiting or outright concealing other options from consideration. Additionally, the default moral status of a social structure is not benevolent, though neither is it necessarily malevolent; the social structure is the emergent result of innumerable helical turns of the morphogenetic cycle, which bakes social interaction (exercises of agency) directly into the process. In this way, some—though not all—actions in relation to a social structure exert causal force on that structure's development and emergence, while other actions are conditioned by the social structure but cannot necessarily exert reciprocal force back onto the structure.

To illustrate this interplay between social structures and ethical agency, Daniel J. Daly analyzes the case of the 2013 collapse of the Rana Plaza sweatshop in Bangladesh.[5] The building's upper floors had been converted by the building's owner, Sohel Rana, to garment factories and outfitted with large generators with the goal of allowing production to continue even during losses of power elsewhere in the city of Dhaka. The day prior to the collapse, cracks appeared in the building, and both workers and an engineer determined the building to be unsafe. However, as Daly explains, "Rana and the owners of the various garment factories in the building urged and then ordered workers to enter the building. Shortly thereafter, the generators were started, which, as usual, caused the structure to shake. This time the shaking caused the building

4. See, for example, the concise history of this problem outlined in Daniel J. Daly, *The Structures of Virtue and Vice* (Georgetown University, 2021), esp. chap. 2.

5. Daly, *The Structures of Virtue and Vice*, 12–13, 202–208.

to buckle and collapse, killing 1,127 people."[6] The disaster sparked an outcry in Bangladesh and the international community,[7] due both to the scale of the loss of life and the preventable nature of that loss.

In cases of avoidable suffering and death like this, questions of who is to blame arise quickly. As Daly points out, clearly the actions of Rana and the owners of the factories played a causal role in the disaster,[8] but the ethical analysis cannot stop there. Social structures were at play that made the Rana Plaza disaster not only thinkable but also likely. Daly calls these *structures of vice*, and names two mutually informing structures operative in twisting the operation of the factories in the Rana Plaza building away from human dignity and flourishing: first, the overwhelming priority of total shareholder return (TSR) in CEO selection and evaluation and second, the relationship between a CEO who is evaluated according to this metric and the owners (like Rana) of factory facilities.[9] Health and flourishing of the factory workers played nearly no part in the relations that governed the day-to-day operation of Rana Plaza,[10] which structurally incentivized an administrative disregard for their safety and very lives.

Structural relations do not stop at industry administration, however. Daly's question moves beyond who is to blame into an analysis of how consumers are implicated in the disaster.[11] Does the act of purchasing clothes made in places like Rana Plaza impute guilt for the disaster into those who purchase them? Daly's answer is no because

---

6. Daly, *The Structures of Virtue and Vice*, 12.

7. See, for example, Joe Westby, "The Rana Plaza Disaster: The Unholy Alliance of Business and Government in Bangladesh, and Around the World," Amnesty International, April 24, 2014, https://www.amnesty.org/en/latest/campaigns/2014/04/rana-plaza-disaster-the-unholy-alliance-of-business-and-government-in-bangladesh-and-around-the-world/.

8. Daly, *The Structures of Virtue and Vice*, 202–203.

9. Daly, *The Structures of Virtue and Vice*, 202–204.

10. Daly, *The Structures of Virtue and Vice*, 204.

11. Daly, *The Structures of Virtue and Vice*. See esp. chap. 1 and 205–207.

an individual refraining from buying a piece of clothing produced in a sweatshop does not exert causal force on the administration of that sweatshop, but Daly also notes that from the perspective of virtue ethics, the question goes beyond moral culpability to questions of character formation: "What kind of person regularly benefits from a web of relations that systematically causes poor garment workers to live diminished lives and suffer a premature death?"[12] Would it not be better—more loving—to work to resist structures of vice like incentivizing attention to profit over human dignity and life by purchasing, so much as one can, items that are less beholden to such structures? Certainly this would be more work and likely more expensive socially and financially—such is the nature of resisting structural conditioning—but this is why Keenan's understanding of sin is so important. Does disregarding the structural harm perpetrated on factory workers in one's purchasing decisions constitute failing to bother to love those workers? Does love not require at least considering the social realities in which they live? In this way, the question of structural sin is not always about culpability; it is about bothering to love.

Where is symbolization in all this? To put it bluntly, symbol is wrapped around the bodies of those who wear clothing produced in factories like the ones in Rana Plaza. Such clothing mediates a multifaceted social reality: affordable clothing obtained as part of a network of structures built to disregard the flourishing of those who produced it. Again, culpability is not the primary question in this; the question is what kind of social reality we build and participate in. Virtue ethics emphasizes that many actions work over time to form the character of a person; those actions also carry a depth of symbolization that coalesces to form the character of a community. Symbolization operates in visibility and legibility; buying, wearing, using particular products or adopting or resisting particular practices interfaces directly with the symbolic depth of a social context.

Another brief example might help to illustrate this. The advent of electric vehicles spearheaded by the Tesla brand and its CEO, Elon Musk,

---

12. Daly, *The Structures of Virtue and Vice*, 205.

initially found a ready and willing consumer base largely on the political left in the United States: "affluent, environmentally-conscious liberals."[13] Driving a Tesla initially came to symbolize, or mediate into the surrounding social reality, the presence of exactly these characteristics—affluence, environmental consciousness, and a certain amount of political progressivism. However, in the years since then, Musk has largely and publicly lurched far to the political right, jarring and even alienating a significant amount of Tesla's core consumer base.[14] Tesla customers have named this as a primary reason for canceling orders,[15] and even current Tesla owners have precipitated a market for bumper stickers printed with slogans like "I bought this before we knew Elon was crazy." The object and its owner do not simply represent or signify something in a social context; they mediate social meaning beyond their own control.

Such symbolized mediations of meaning can be remarkably socially resilient, particularly if they are negative. Take, for example, the 2006 raids by the US Immigration and Customs Enforcement (ICE) on meat-processing plants owned by Swift & Co. throughout the Midwest of the United States.[16] At that time, it was the largest ICE raid in US history, and it jolted the social realities of the communities—many rural or small—in which it took place. Worthington, Minnesota (population of roughly thirteen thousand), the county seat of rural Nobles County, was one community in which ICE raided a processing plant. The raid largely

13. Ryan Cooper, "Elon Musk and the Decline of Tesla," *American Prospect*, June 17, 2024, https://prospect.org/power/2024-06-17-elon-musk-decline-of-tesla/#:~:text=dealerships%20this%20year.-,In%20the%20first%20quarter%20of%20this%20year%2C%20Tesla%20sales%20slumped,namely%20affluent%2C%20environmentally%20conscious%20liberals.

14. Ian Sherr, "Tesla Drivers Are Getting Fed Up with Elon Musk's Twitter Meltdowns," CNET, December 23, 2022, https://www.cnet.com/tech/tesla-drivers-are-getting-fed-up-with-elon-musks-twitter-meltdowns/.

15. Scherr, "Tesla Drivers."

16. See Jerry Kammer, "The 2006 Swift Raids: Assessing the Impact of Immigration Enforcement Actions at Six Facilities," Center for Immigration Studies, March 18, 2009, https://cis.org/Report/2006-Swift-Raids.

targeted Latine workers and did not discriminate between US citizens and noncitizens, leading to situations of family separation and social turmoil.[17] The responses of the Worthington community took on a character more evocative of disaster response than of affirmation of government authority. Churches became places of shelter for those who felt unsafe returning to their homes or for children whose parents had been detained.[18] Community organizers and members of religious communities collaborated to form the Worthington Area Immigration Advocates (WAIA) network, focusing on building relationships with migrant persons and providing legal assistance.[19] The necessity of a community response was more than simply logistical or pragmatic; the processing plant was a central pillar of the community, and support for those affected by ICE's raid on the plant was a symbolizing practice many saw as necessary, interpreted as "good old-fashioned Midwestern neighborliness."[20] An action by a governmental structure perpetrated harm on members of this community, and the responses of support went beyond individual ones to the communal. In doing so, the responses underwent symbolization, mediating in the concrete life of the community what neighborliness means.

The effects of this symbolization proliferated for the next decade and a half in Worthington, laying a symbolized protostructural groundwork for what would become the community's response to the COVID-19 pandemic in 2020 and following. In a community rocked by a disruptive governmental raid, one might expect hesitation to cooperate with governmental initiatives aimed at stemming the spread of COVID-19. Additionally, Worthington was an early epicenter of

17. See, for example, Mark Steil, "Meat-Packing Plant Loses Workers to Immigration Raid," NPR, December 13, 2006, https://www.npr.org/2006/12/13/6620724/meat-packing-plant-loses-workers-to-immigration-raid.

18. Steil, "Meat-Packing Plant."

19. Randy Capps and Michael Fix, "Changing the Playbook: Immigrants and the COVID-19 Response in Two U.S. Communities," Migration Policy Institute, July 2022, 1–2. https://www.migrationpolicy.org/sites/default/files/publications/mpi_covid19-immigrant-communities_final.pdf.

20. Capps and Fix, "Changing the Playbook," 15.

COVID-19 infection. Because the meat-processing plant still played a large employing role in the city, a large portion of the town's labor force (estimated to be close to 80 percent)[21] was deemed to consist of "essential workers" who continued to work through the onset and unfolding of the pandemic. Social structures were certainly at play in this; the processing plant sat at the nexus of influential social relations between hog farmers who needed to get their livestock processed and consumers who needed the meat. Additionally, many workers (documented and not) named a fear of lost wages as a primary reason for needing to continue working in the plant through the pandemic.[22]

My point is not about these structures of employment and production, however; my point is about the structures of trust and community that endured following the responses to the 2006 ICE raid. The work of structures like WAIA and Unidos Minnesota helped facilitate impressively successful mass testing and vaccination programs in Worthington, efforts that were able to include the migrant members of the community in large part because of relationships of trust that had been taking root for the past fourteen years.[23] This kind of community cohesion resists instrumentalist interpretation. What was exchanged between community members in 2006 was more than assistance; it was gifts of solidary neighborliness, symbolic exchanges that spoke in the key of symbolization, not signification. The members of Worthington in this way gave and received *each other*, crafting a social reality whose symbolic depth constituted a deep reservoir from which to draw a response to the subsequent disaster of the COVID-19 pandemic.

Symbol and Race in Rural America

Unfortunately, not all stories of structural harm transform into neighborly community symbolization like that found in Worthington. All

21. Capps and Fix, "Changing the Playbook," 13.

22. Capps and Fix, "Changing the Playbook," 13–16.

23. Capps and Fix, "Changing the Playbook," 12–19.

too often, sinful structures precipitate inhumanity and are inoculated against social change or reform by overlapping symbolizations that compete to confuse or convert the contextual narrative away from sin or evil and toward twisted conceptions of necessity, pragmatism, or misplaced solidarity. The toxicity of sinful social structures—those that, in Finn's words, "encourage morally evil actions"[24]—extends well beyond the particular instances of harm they cultivate. The effects of sinful structures include normalizing structuralized risks of harm, an effect that is often mirrored in cases of structures that are ethically ambivalent rather than unambiguously sinful—those that can, depending on context and circumstance, catalyze both social benefits and social harms. In such cases, symbolization of the ethically ambivalent social structures speaks in simultaneous, discordant tones, mediating multiple social realities into contexts where those overlapping realities may precipitate unrest, conflict, and retraumatization of the persons and communities harmed.

In rural American contexts, the symbolizing work of sinful social structures can be masked by the very social self-understanding that characterizes them: the local moral community. The moral community is exactly what many rural folks experience as *good* about rural life: its connotations of belonging, feeling at home, knowing and appreciating the local values and customs, and so on. However, what makes the rural moral community what it is, is exactly the primacy of the local—of neighborliness and accountability to those who are physically proximate. Values like solidarity, then, first and foremost play out in many rural contexts as solidarity with vulnerable persons *here*, in this particular local place—not necessarily because the moral community prefers itself to others[25] but because the moral community mediates individual and communal identity. The moral community in this way is a symbol in addition to being a social conception; it mediates social reality in ways that are not reducible to signification or instrumentalization. The moral

24. Finn, "What Is a Sinful Social Structure?" 155.

25. Recall this disambiguation in relation to problematic comments from JD Vance in note 215 above.

community symbolizes—mediates—a social world, a context within which inhere the primary referents of solidarity and the common good.

Problems can arise when solidary action with those in one's rural moral community competes with a moral call to solidarity with non-local persons or those who are not viewed as "local." Such moral calls can often include acting in solidarity with those experiencing social suffering or oppression but who are not readily regarded as part of a local moral community by those who exercise significant power and influence in the moral community. In Minnesota, this was thrown into sharp relief in 2020 following the murder of George Floyd by a police officer. Rural conceptions of law enforcement often focus on its beneficial structural aspects, but in Daly's analysis of the operative structures, the field of law enforcement contains both "structures of virtue and structures of vice . . . Because of their social positions, police officers are enabled and are required to, for example, protect individuals from domestic abusers. This constitutes a virtuous relation among social positions insofar as the structure is designed to promote the well-being of survivors. However, there are vicious relations embedded in the social structure of law enforcement. The repeated killings of unarmed African Americans at the hands of on-duty police officers requires people of conscience to investigate the agential and social factors that give rise to this systemic social injustice."[26] Daly specifically cites the murder of Floyd, a Black man, as an evil facilitated by vicious structures in law enforcement, including the tendency of police unions (social structures themselves) to protect officers who abuse Black persons and the socialization of officers to "devalue Black lives and to follow norms that justify the use of physical and often deadly force against Black individuals."[27]

Daly's analysis of the structural evils at play in the murder of George Floyd is helpful, as well as others',[28] but the symbolizing repercussions

26. Daly, *The Structures of Virtue and Vice*, 183.

27. Daly, *The Structures of Virtue and Vice*, 184–185.

28. See, for example, Carolyn M. Jones Medine, "Womanist Spirit and Womanist Healing for Sandra Bland and George Floyd," *Black Women and Religious Cultures*

that subsequently echoed through rural contexts bring an added layer of complexity. In the wake of Floyd's murder, parts of Minnesota and the wider United States erupted in protests, while other parts of the state and nation, particularly in rural areas, recoiled from what they interpreted as rioting. These communities often fell into counternarratives of "backing the blue" and other similar attempts to show support for law enforcement. My suggestion is that one important part of this recoil, in rural areas specifically, was the result of the collision of competing symbolizations of solidarity, and another important part was the operation of whiteness in and on the public imagination of what it means to be rural—as Conn rightly notes, "Whiteness has always been a central part of our rural mythology."[29] On the one hand was the horrific murder of Floyd at the hands of police, demanding solidary action with those who continue to be at greatest risk of police brutality. On the other hand, in many rural conceptions, were local neighbors who *were* members of law enforcement, many of whom were similarly appalled by Floyd's murder. Much of the national conversation, however, could not accommodate this nuance; it largely became a question of whether one stood in solidarity with Black communities or supported law enforcement. Each largely symbolized the exclusion of the other.

At least in Minnesota, that perceived incompatibility translated into many rural spaces filling with thin-blue-line flags and stickers in car windows. This is in no way to suggest that such a reaction was acceptable or just; rather, it is symbolically legible—and symbols, as protostructures, share the potential of social structures to be sinful. Within many rural moral communities, interpretations of what it meant to be a good rural neighbor grew first from what it meant to support the local police

1, no. 1 (2020): 89–107; Rita Nakashima Brock, "The Pandemic Paradox: George Floyd, Moral Injury, and the Sustainability of Social Movements," in *Doing Theology in Pandemics: Facing Viruses, Violence, and Vitriol*, ed. Zachary Moon (Pickwick, 2022), 1–14; or Ayanna Grady-Hunt, "Larcenia Floyd and Representations of the Divine: The Path to Justice Is Black, Feminine, and Interfaith," *Berkeley Journal of Religion and Theology* 6, no. 1 (2020): 4–9.

29. Conn, *The Lies of the Land*, 254.

officers known locally by name, and by extension the structures their work symbolized, before questions of being a good neighbor to Black community members were entertained. To the extent that such support of one's law-enforcement neighbors also mediated a denial of solidarity with a vulnerable population, such a denial became itself the focus of reactionary denials, re-explanations, and attempts to reinterpret the social impact of rural support for law enforcement. Tropes of law and order reemerged as commonplace in rural discourses, laid out alongside suggestions that to critique systems operative in law enforcement was tantamount to hate-mongering. As one resident of rural Albany, Minnesota, wrote in a local newspaper, "When did we start judging whole groups like police on the conduct of a few? . . . As a blue-collar, proud, U.S. veteran and Christian, I'm ashamed that people are pushing hate."[30]

To be clear, responses from rural America were not unified in this. Even the column just cited was part of a zealous back-and-forth disagreement between rural residents. On the whole, however, it was a rare thing to drive through rural Minnesota and see a Black Lives Matter sign and a relatively common one to see the thin-blue-line flag. Symbols mediated a social atmosphere in which multiple discordant meanings were made manifest.

There is at least one significant moral problem with this symbolic legibility. The operative self-understanding of many rural spaces in Minnesota prioritized standing with the structurally visible local embodiments of law enforcement, with relatively little acknowledgment that in nearly all rural spaces, Black residents *are also local*—a fact obscured by the operation of whiteness on many popular perceptions of rural America. Solidarity with Black persons and other persons of color is not a nonlocal concern for much of rural America; rural demographics in the United States have been increasingly nonwhite for some

30. Kevin Hall, "West Words Had It Right, Not Wrong," *Morrison County Record*, June 19, 2020, https://www.hometownsource.com/morrison_county_record/west-words-had-it-right-not-wrong/article_96dc06d4-b28b-11ea-8483-8706486dec96.html.

time now.[31] That it was often *perceived* that way bespeaks entanglement of rural symbolization with the sins of white supremacy and racism.[32] The thin-blue-line flags and other similar symbolizations mediated a kind of support for law enforcement, but they did so contextually by *also* and *simultaneously* mediating bigotry—not in the perception of many who flew them in their yards or stuck them in their vehicle windows but to those (especially persons of color and allies) for whom such symbolization wrote them out of their own local moral community. Symbolization can mediate multiple social realities at the same time, and rarely are they all ethically resonant.

This example looms large here not in an effort to excuse or defend particular practices of symbolization, or even to reduce such practices to only those meanings listed here, but to begin to indicate the ways that the symbolization of the rural moral community can blend with sinful social realities. In a word, whiteness can easily find symbolized expression in the practices of moral community. By *whiteness*, I do not mean phenotypical skin pigmentation or a lack thereof. I mean instead what Bryan Massingale explains as "a social group that has access to political, social, economic, or cultural advantages that people of color do not share."[33] It is not ethically problematic to have a particular skin pigmentation; it is ethically problematic to enjoy advantages connected to that skin pigmentation that are denied to those who do not share it.

The connection of whiteness to the rural moral community runs through the history of its conceptual development. In his seminal text *The Christian Imagination: Theology and the Origins of Race*, Willie James Jennings explains that the development of the concept (and social reality) of whiteness went hand in hand with the supersessionist

31. See D. W. Rowlands and Hannah Love, "Mapping Rural America's Diversity and Demographic Change," Brookings, September 28, 2021, https://www.brookings.edu/articles/mapping-rural-americas-diversity-and-demographic-change/.

32. For a more developed picture of the nexus between whiteness and rural political realities in the United States, see Thomas F. Schaller and Tom Waldman, *White Rural Rage: The Threat to American Democracy* (Random House, 2024).

33. Bryan Massingale, *Racial Justice and the Catholic Church* (Orbis, 2010), 2.

and colonizing expansion of Christianity.[34] As European Christians worked to theologically justify their colonizing power over native peoples in the so-called New World, the conception of what it *is* to be a people became untethered from identification with a particular place or land.[35] If the German people belonged to the physical land of Germany, and the Italian people belonged to the physical land of Italy, then the Indigenous peoples of the New World would be those who belong to the land of the New World. That would mean, however, that they had a legitimate claim to the land, which was untenable in a colonizing mindset. To mitigate this problem, the social machine of colonization excised social identity from land and sutured it instead to European Christendom. In the vacuum of social identifiability dictated by land, the concept of whiteness emerged. To be white meant to be privy to Christian colonizing power, defined in terms of relationships to European powers of Christendom, *not* in relation to particular lands or locations. In Jennings's words, "Whiteness replaced the earth as the signifier of identities. It would be a mistake to see this replacement as a discursive practice fully controlled by Europeans. It *is* a discursive practice, but one that presented itself as the only real option given the aggressive desacralization of the world. When you disrupt and destroy the delicate and contingent connection of peoples' identities bound to specific lands you leave no alternative but racial agency."[36] It is essential to note the religious content of this early development of whiteness. Jennings's insistence that analyzing whiteness "requires nothing less than a theological consideration"[37] is part of what distinguishes his analysis of race from other secular theorists. Within many areas of theology, his perspective has become authoritative, leading theologians like Jeannine Hill Fletcher to concur that "European Christians surveyed

34. Willie James Jennings, *The Christian Imagination: Theology and the Origins of Race* (Yale University, 2010). See esp. chap. 1.

35. Jennings, *The Christian Imagination*, 57–59.

36. Jennings, *The Christian Imagination*, 58.

37. Jennings, *The Christian Imagination*, 290.

the non-Christian other with disdain . . . With a racial hierarchy as part of the natural order of things, non-White, non-Christian others were assessed to be deficient on a sliding scale of humanity."[38] Put differently, social identities that mattered most came to be those most closely associated with white, Christian identities.

This conception of whiteness connects to symbolizations operative in rural America through the tendency to scale what is socially determinative along lines determined by whiteness. Because in this set of understandings, "white" does not connote simply a phenotype but rather a social group with unique advantages, its impact transcends and includes the racial. Whiteness is not simply about race, though that is certainly an integral part of it; it is also about having access to social structures that are likely to have favorable rather than unfavorable impacts based on the social group to which one belongs. The Albany resident's allusion to Christian identity as a relevant part of American identity is in this way not accidental. It is an unsurprising consequence of inhabiting an American context that is roughly three-quarters white and four-fifths Christian.[39] Additionally, many rural reactions to the murder of George Floyd indicate a de-identification of many rural moral communities with their residents of color. That there are notable deviations from this (such as the solidarity exhibited in Worthington in reaction to ICE raids focused on their Latine residents) tends to demonstrate the rule by way of exception.

Whiteness, then, is an order of symbols that tends to mediate parts of rural social reality as a function of their social proximity to a symbolic white, Christian ideal. This does not mean that whiteness or white supremacy is therefore determinative of *all* aspects of rural moral community. Rather, the sins of white supremacy, racism, xenophobia,

38. Jeannine Hill Fletcher, *The Sin of White Supremacy: Christianity, Racism, and Religious Diversity in America* (Orbis, 2017), 9–10. See also Katie Walker Grimes, *Christ Divided: Antiblackness as Corporate Vice* (Fortress, 2017).

39. Rowlands and Love, "Mapping"; and Public Religion Research Institute and American Communities Project Staff, "Religious Stereotypes vs. Reality in Urban, Suburban, and Rural America."

and other social sins can infect rural moral community through the symbolic order just as they are threats to nonrural communities. It is not simply happenstance that white Christian nationalism finds a ready home in many rural areas.[40] Nor is it socially befuddling that anti-Muslim speakers have regularly charted courses through rural areas.[41] When locality is a primary determining factor in constituting the home of a moral community, how such locality is determined carries real social consequences mediated through the symbolization of that moral community. In this implicit social calculus, questions of locality tend to hold sway: Which is more local—law enforcement or the Black community? Which has more of a claim on the identity of a rural moral community—white Christian nationalism or religious and racial diversity? Questions like these are not adjudicated monolithically, nor do the answers necessarily remain constant in particular rural contexts; they *are*, however, structurally and symbolically influenced, meaning that social-ethical evaluation of how they take shape in rural contexts must also exhibit symbolic and structural literacy.

Symbolic Reductionism

When sin twists symbolization in rural social reality, it can do so in ways that go beyond prescribing membership and nonmembership in a moral community. One common malformation of the symbolic order is

40. Lisa Hagen, "Christian Nationalism's Support Is Strongest in Rural, Conservative States," NPR, February 28, 2024, https://www.npr.org/2024/02/28/1234304058/christian-nationalism-survey. See also the original study: "Support for Christian Nationalism in All 50 States: Findings from PRRI's 2023 American Values Atlas," *PRRI*, February 28, 2024, https://www.prri.org/research/support-for-christian-nationalism-in-all-50-states/.

41. Matt McKinney, "Anti-Muslim Speaking Circuit Runs Through Rural Minnesota," *Star Tribune*, April 17, 2016, https://www.startribune.com/anti-muslim-speaking-circuit-runs-through-rural-minnesota/375924701. See also John Enger, "Anti-Islam Speakers Urge Rural MN Crowds to Prepare for Muslim Attack," *MPRNews*, October 25, 2016, https://www.mprnews.org/story/2016/10/25/antiislam-speakers-urge-rural-mn-prepare-muslim-attack.

to reduce complex human realities into inadequate but easily identifiable denotations and then allow those denotations to carry ever-increasing social-symbolizing weight, a process that can be called *symbolic reductionism*. In treating complex human realities as something less than they are, and subsequently allowing those treatments to monopolistically symbolize the human realities they inadequately portray, symbolic reductionism carries an inherent dehumanizing tendency, stacking it against human dignity and flourishing. Stereotyping, of course, also does this, but stereotyping finds *voice* in particular symbols and symbolizations; it is not *itself* symbolization. Symbolic reductionism, then, is mediation of a cheapened social reality, the gift of a false coin wherein what is given is no longer beyond value; it has been emptied of value.

An example of symbolic reductionism would be overzealous fixation on a particular issue or problem, imbuing that issue or problem with symbolic meaning that it can carry only by isolating itself from other issues that ought also to participate in mediating social reality. Single-issue politics tends to do this, and in many rural American contexts, there is no single issue that has held sway in recent decades like that of abortion. To be clear, the point in this discussion is *not* to critique or defend the legal availability or moral permissibility of abortion itself; the point is to recognize that in rural contexts where abortion has become, for many practical purposes, the *only* relevant political issue, such exclusive attention can precipitate symbolic reductionism, flattening the mediation of social reality to only that filtered through the lens of this issue. Then, when social structures are built and rebuilt through actions such as voting and legislation, the full view of the common good has been compromised, skewed to being mediated by this one dominant symbolizing issue. Abortion is a moral, ethical, and political issue, but it has also operated as a symbol, and when symbols reduce rather than mediate the depth and breadth of social reality—or more correctly, when they mediate *by* reduction—they inhibit access to the full truth of social reality with all its ethical challenges. In this way, symbolic reductionism is a protostructure that inhibits an adequate grasp of the social reality one inhabits. It also inhibits the practice of love, a practice ordered toward the particular humans who make up that complex social reality. In a word, symbolic reductionism is sinful; it inhibits the ability to bother to love.

To develop the example of abortion a bit more fully, one should note that opposition to abortion is obviously not unique to rural areas in the United States. However, rural contexts do tend to have a higher percentage of residents opposed to abortion than do nonrural ones. According to Wuthnow, "Compared to cities of at least 250,000, the odds of opposing abortion in the smallest towns are more than three times higher."[42] This does not mean that symbolic reductionism is operative in all these contexts, but it does indicate that there is a concentration of similar perspectives in these contexts that can facilitate the proliferation of symbolic reductionism if given the chance. Wuthnow's study of rural Kansas is illuminative here.[43] He describes four discernible positions of rural folks regarding abortion in Kansas and other states in 2009. First, there were activists, especially rural clergy, who took on leadership roles in crafting social opposition to abortion. Second, there were residents who opposed abortion but did not take part in the same kinds of activism, those who "generally summarized their view succinctly, almost as if they had declared themselves against abortion so many times that they were weary of discussing the topic despite feeling strongly about it."[44] Third were those who were pro-choice but who were also "reluctant to express their opinions locally,"[45] and finally was the group of folks who "were just tired of the issue. It was the elephant in the room that kept dominating discussions at church and in politics. They not only wanted it to be resolved, to go away somehow, but were

42. Wuthnow, *The Left Behind*, 123. See also Robert Wuthnow, *Small-Town America: Finding Community, Shaping the Future* (Princeton University, 2013), 269.

43. Wuthnow, *The Left Behind*, 124–127. See also Wuthnow, *Red State Religion*.

44. Wuthnow, *The Left Behind*, 125.

45. Wuthnow, *The Left Behind*, 127.

also disdainful of people who took strong vocal stands on it one way or the other."[46]

This last group is an indicator of symbolic reductionism. There are other indicators as well, like the fatigue of those opposed to abortion or the socially sanctioned silence of those who were pro-choice, but the clear presence of a group whose position on abortion centered not on its *permissibility* but on its *domination of discourse* suggests the issue had taken on a symbolizing role that reduced rather than facilitated mediation of the full, complex social reality the group inhabits. Such symbolization mediates real social interactions—the second step of critical realist sociology's morphogenetic cycle—in ways that constrict or prevent attention to other relevant issues that have been filtered out of social awareness by symbolic reductionism. As theologian Emily Reimer-Barry noted in 2019, reflecting on whether it is possible or feasible to oppose abortion and also attend to other moral issues, "I have been attending Catholic Mass for three years at a parish eight miles from the U.S.-Mexico border, and I have never heard a homily on immigration, inhumane detention facilities, or Customs and Border Patrol family separation policies. Despite the fact that children are dying in Immigration and Customs Enforcement (ICE) custody, abortion seems to be the only 'life' issue the pastor and deacons wish to address from the pulpit."[47] Reimer-Barry's liturgically centered example drawn from her experience highlights the connection between symbolic reductionism as a social symptom and its ritual manifestations. Wuthnow, too, notes the role of ritual religious practice in rural discourse about and attention to abortion.[48] As we saw earlier, ritual does not claim exclusive dominion over the symbolic order, but it is a privileged place where the symbolic order speaks and forms its context. As such, liturgical symbolization

46. Wuthnow, *The Left Behind*, 127.

47. Emily Reimer-Barry, "Another Pro-Life Movement Is Possible," *CTSA Proceedings* 74 (2019): 21–22.

48. Wuthnow, *The Left Behind*, 124–129. See also Robert Wuthnow, *Religion's Power: What Makes It Work* (Oxford University, 2023), esp. chap. 1.

plays a key role whether a Christian context facilitates or resists symbolic reductionism. Preaching itself is a structured symbolic role, connected to the gathered liturgical assembly, of which Robert Hovda famously claimed, writing at the time for the US Catholic Bishops' Committee on the Liturgy, "Among the symbols with which the liturgy deals, none is more important than this assembly of believers."[49] Part of the assembly's symbolization is mediating the symbolic order into the social context; when symbol falls into sin liturgically (whether symbolic reductionism or another sinful form), the results can be disastrous.[50]

Single-issue politics is not the only form symbolic reductionism can take. Symbolic reductionism can also operate by mediating strife or discord or by conversely mediating idolization of particular ways of thinking, acting, or believing. Social conflict or even social anger is not inherently sinful,[51] but if social conflicts or angers are mediated through symbolizations that artificially reduce rather than evoke the realities they mediate, the symbolized reduction takes on a sinfulness resonant with that of overzealous fixation on single issues: It inhibits rather than facilitates full, genuine encounter with a social context and the persons who constitute it.

Perhaps the most straightforward way by which to illustrate symbolic reductionism through discord and strife is political polarization and partisan tribalism. Diversity of opinion and even competing approaches to the common good are not necessarily sinful simply because they are not the same. Such is the stuff of much of the field of social ethics. However, words and concepts can be twisted to mediate

49. Bishops' Committee on the Liturgy, *Environment and Art in Catholic Worship* (United States Catholic Conference), 1978, para. 28. See also Bryan Cones, *This Assembly of Believers: The Gifts of Difference in the Church at Prayer* (SCM Press, 2020).

50. See Turnbloom, "Liturgy in the Shadow of Trauma," and Karst, "Caught in the Act."

51. Michael P. Jaycox has argued convincingly to the contrary; see Michael P. Jaycox, "The Civic Virtues of Social Anger: A Critically Reconstructed Normative Ethic for Public Life," *Journal of the Society of Christian Ethics* 36, no. 1 (2016): 123–143.

a symbolic depth that is dominated by social discord in such a way that *only* the discord speaks. Discord can then become bloated enough to crowd out all other symbolization (and signification, for that matter), reducing the discourse to a meaning far shallower and less accurate than it otherwise would have been.

A few years ago, I was invited to give a talk on Catholic social teaching in a rural Minnesota parish. It was an interesting event, as the audience was made up of middle-school-aged children and their parents, inviting consideration not only of how to connect with both present age groups but also of how to navigate the evaluative expectations of the parents. As the event unfolded, everyone was friendly and welcoming, the staff was very helpful and supportive, and on the whole it was a positive experience, with the exception of one slipup I made during the presentation. I was explaining as best I could concepts like the common good, human dignity, solidarity, and subsidiarity, and during one of the explanations, I used the term *social justice*. Immediately as I did so, there was a chilling effect in the room. Some parents shifted in their seats uncomfortably, and I got more than one disapproving look. It was a term I had resolved not to use for exactly this reason; the context I was visiting was, at the time, one in which the term *social justice* symbolized leftwing, liberal ideology, an unwelcome mediation in that place. More specifically, it was not necessarily just the perceived liberalness of the term *social justice* that offended folks, though perhaps that was part of it too; it was the injection of what was received as inflammatory language—language that made present contextual political strife—into a pedagogical space that grated on the attendees.

The presentation moved on, and the audience seemed to more or less forgive me for my misstep, but the point here is that while I had no intention of mediating political strife or discord into the presentation, the term *social justice* symbolized that anyway. I *knew* this would likely be the case going in, and so it was relatively easy to change vocabulary, but consider if I had missed the contextual cues. The meaning I was trying to express with the term *social justice* would have been reduced to its partisan symbolism, and the symbolic bloat of that partisan meaning would have swollen to obscure the whole event. In none of this am I assigning any blame—recall that culpability is a tenuous thing when speaking of structures. The point is simply that the term *social justice* connoted a protostructure of political strife, and the social interaction resisted that protostructural gesturing.

The way this interfaces with sinfulness is that a term like *social justice* does not need to be reduced to only this specific mediation of meaning (that of political discord or polarization). When its symbolization is reduced in this way, it deprives the community of the rich theological and conceptual history of the term, particularly in the Roman Catholic tradition, which in turn inhibits the full flourishing of the community into the very religious identity in which it was explicitly trying to grow. The sinfulness is not by the agency of the community; it is in the emergent symbolic reductionism precipitated by a toxic political climate.

Symbolic reductionism can also unfold by limiting what are perceived as "correct" ways of acting to only those that resonate with socially powerful entities in a community. Put differently, this is the problem with what is sometimes called *common sense* in rural moral communities. Common sense—and adherence to it—is not itself necessarily morally suspect; in fact, it is an important component in the makeup of the moral community. What makes good sense in a particular context, especially a rural one, is socially conditioned—held in common—by those who make such a context their home. Common sense at its best mediates practices that are beneficial to both individuals and the communities they inhabit, imbuing its contexts with an affect of home and shared values.

Where symbolic reductionism can twist common sense, however, is when common sense is inflated to become the *only conceivable way* of thinking or acting rightly, and any deviation from it is treated as self-evidently wrong. The problem with this reduction of moral calculus to contextually mediated common sense is that common sense resists evaluation beyond the sensibilities of those who view themselves to hold it, and it is rarely as cohesive as the fantasy of common sense suggests. At its worst, common sense morphs simply into judgmentalism, whereby bystanders and observers of a set of actions become evaluators of the action, referees thumping the imagined rule book of common sense. This is a particular problem in rural and small-town contexts, where famously everyone is perceived to know everyone else's business. Common sense can become something of a spectator sport, discerning and reevaluating the rules based on the social dynamics of community observation and storytelling. Such a morphology can denigrate the moral agency of those directly involved in actions that the community then retells and evaluates, obscuring the difficulties and complexities of human moral discernment. Common sense, if misappropriated or misused, can mediate the reduction of human situations to judgment problems, acting as an inhibitor to efforts to bother to love. Common sense is not necessarily sinful, but it can facilitate sin if it is twisted by symbolic reductionism.

Lying Symbols

The symbolic order, as a pole of language opposite that of sign, shares in the possibility of all language to speak untruth just as it can speak truth. Symbols can, in a sense, lie. They can mediate meanings that are untrue, and they can obscure or omit relevant meanings that are true. One might revisit an objection that opened this chapter, that the symbol itself, as a protostructure, lacks agency or consciousness just as social structures do and is therefore incapable of the action of lying. Strictly speaking, this is correct. However, herein lies an important distinction between social structures and symbols: Social structures are networks of relations, and by their organization of social relations, they inhibit or facilitate particular ways of acting.[52] Symbols, on the other hand, are mediations of social reality that gesture toward structures, and they can continue mediating social reality far after agential action has ceased. If an agent—an individual or communal entity—facilitates

52. Finn, "What Is a Sinful Social Structure?"

the symbolization of a lie, that symbolized untruth can echo through social reality with great resilience and vitality, sustained by communal participation in and affirmation of the symbolized untruth. It is in this sense that symbols can lie; they can mediate untruth in a key of non-value, of noninstrumentalization, of gift. If a gift is untrue, what can it be called but a lie?

Chapter 1 included Stanton's description of competing narratives of the rural. He points out convincingly that each narrative falls short of capturing the full truth of rural America[53] stops short of arguing that the narratives mediate untruth. To be sure, there is nothing wrong with offering limited or partial views of social truth—*all* views of social truth are necessarily partial—but the problem posed by symbolization, in particular, is that partial mediations of social truth can be received in good faith as more than they are, crowding out other equally true, equally partial mediations of social truth.

An example, part of the symbolic makeup of narratives surrounding rural and small-town America is that there is a kind of safety in the moral community. It is where one feels at home, after all, conditioned by networks of reciprocal responsibility and shared values. Additionally, the symbol of small-town or rural safety speaks at least some level of statistical truth; violent crime generally takes place at lower rates in rural areas than nonrural ones, and property crime likewise tends to occur at a lower rate in rural areas.[54] When I taught ethics at a community college in central Minnesota, we would nearly always do a brief unit on social problems in small towns since many of the students came from surrounding rural areas and small communities and would likely return to them for their professional and family lives. A mainstay in this unit was, after content and trigger warnings, an in-depth exposé published by a local newspaper detailing human trafficking that took place in the

53. Stanton, *Reclaiming Rural*, chap. 1.

54. US Department of Justice, Office of Justice Programs, Bureau of Justice Statistics, *Criminal Victimization, 2022* (September 2023), 9, table 8, https://bjs.ojp.gov/document/cv22.pdf.

surrounding rural areas and small communities.[55] Nearly without fail, students' reactions of disgust and moral outrage, justified as they were, were not limited to offense that such crimes could take place *at all*; they regularly included offense at the idea that such crimes could take place *here*, in these small communities where everyone knows everyone and people were supposed to be responsible for one another, where folks were supposed to look out for one another.

The symbol of rural, small-town safety then, depending on how it is received, can mediate untruth. The lie that small-town safety prevents anything like human trafficking from taking place in rural areas is an attractive one. It resonates with narratives like the idyllic country paradise that Stanton examines and critiques, and symbolizations like the rural moral community. However, it remains an untruth because it precludes consideration of the whole truth, and if it is given an outsized symbolic weight, it can mediate an account of rural social reality that erases those who are victimized. This is the danger of lying symbols; conceptions of what is socially possible and socially actual are mediated not only by data and statistics but also by symbolization. It is true that rural communities, just like nonrural ones, *should not* be places where human trafficking is possible or actual, but it is untrue that they *are not* places where such crime is possible and actual. The space between *should not* and *are not* is mediated in part by lying symbols, mediations of untruth that can operate nearly unrecognized in those who have received them.

The example of rural human trafficking as opposed to perceived rural safety is a sobering one, but not all symbolized untruths mediate an inaccurately positive perception of their content. Recall that the other narrative Stanton critiques is that of the rural being locked in a pattern of decline and decay, something that is likewise not necessarily true. One of the most influential articulations of this narrative comes from Patrick J. Carr and Maria J. Kefalas in their book *Hollowing Out the Middle: The Rural Brain Drain and What It Means for America*, in

---

55. Jenny Berg, Stephanie Dickrell, and David Unze, "Sex Trafficking: The Victims Next Door," *SC Times*, July 21, 2016, https://www.sctimes.com/story/news/local/2016/07/21/sex-trafficking-victims-next-door/87248556/.

which the authors lay out what they see as a crisis for rural social sustainability.[56] As they explain it, rural communities are socially structured to lose their most promising talents, especially among their youth, to other social contexts. In their words, "Small towns play an unwitting part in their own decline. Teachers, parents, and neighbors feel obligated to push and prod the talented kids to succeed, yet, when their best and brightest follow their advice, the investment the community has made in them becomes a boon for someplace else, while the remaining young people are neither afforded the same attention nor groomed for success of any kind."[57] A more stinging critique of rural social stewardship would be difficult to find. This narrative has made it into the popular and professional imagination regarding rural America, finding voice in everything from novels and TV shows to sociological works like those from Wuthnow.[58] It speaks with a kind of thunderous authority: Rural life is doomed to decline, prevented from thriving by its own formation of talent for exodus.

And yet, whether or not their assessment was completely true in 2009 when Carr and Kefalas published their work (even prior to 2009 there was some question of whether the rural brain drain was real or illusory),[59] since then there has emerged a sustained counternarrative—somewhat coyly termed the "rural brain gain"—that argues many rural areas are actually seeing influxes of talent and expertise.[60] The difficulty of navigating between these two counternarratives runs deeper than

56. Patrick J. Carr and Maria J. Kefalas, *Hollowing Out the Middle: The Rural Brain Drain and What It Means for America* (Beacon, 2009).

57. Carr and Kefalas, *Hollowing Out the Middle*, 24.

58. Wuthnow, *The Left Behind*, 56–60.

59. Georgeanne Artz, "Rural Area Brain Drain: Is It a Reality?" *Choices: A Publication of the American Agricultural Economics Association* (4th Quarter 2003): 11–15.

60. Ben Winchester, "A Rural Brain Gain Migration," University of Minnesota Extension, accessed March 18, 2025, https://extension.umn.edu/economic-development/rural-brain-gain-migration. See also Ilana Newman, "'Brain Gain' in Rural America and Who Is Behind It," *Daily Yonder*, March 13, 2024, https://dailyyonder.com/brain-gain-in-rural-america-and-who-is-behind-it/2024/03/13/.

interpretation of data. The symbolic weight of the brain drain exerts social influence in both rural self-conceptions and nonrural conceptions of the rural, regardless of its congruence or incongruence with the lived experiences of many rural communities. In a word, the symbolic damage has been done, and even rural communities that may be thriving nevertheless carry the impact of this symbolism—even if *they* are thriving now, many other rural communities must not be, and their thriving is by no means assured or stable. The brain drain mediates symbolism of social precariousness more or less independent of whether rural communities actually experience such precariousness.

We saw some of this in our studies of rural Minnesotan Christian congregations. Exactly zero of our interviewees described their experience of the local church or their local community as precarious or in unavoidable decline; many actually described quite the opposite. Interviewees often spoke in proud terms of stable social life in their community, sustained in part by participation in their church community, friend and family relationships, and longevity of their community membership. When interviewees did speak of decline, they did so always in reference either to *other* communities or to a general perception of nonlocalized decline or exodus. One church youth leader, after describing how they experienced their church community as hope-filled and healthy, expressed worry about the community perception held by more elderly members of the congregation: "They [the elderly members] read the stats of how many people are leaving high school and not going to church anymore and those things, and so they see the need and they want to care, but I don't know if they're necessarily hopeful that something will change."[61] That there is a perceived need that "something will change" at all, when one's experience is already of a healthy and hope-filled community, suggests the social potency of the brain drain symbolization even in rural contexts where it is not experienced as a problem firsthand. Further, in the perception of this interviewee, it was "the stats"—data—that occasioned the brain drain symbolization. It is a symbolization that, even if it holds true at some

61. Anonymized interviewee, interviewed by Lydia Mattern, summer 2022.

times and in some places, can also mediate untruth at other times and in other places. Just as it is harmful to imbibe a falsely positive view of a social context, it can be harmful to imbibe a falsely negative one. In both cases, perceiving social reality goes beyond the discursive; symbols themselves can mediate untruth.

Conclusion

This chapter has unpacked some of the ways symbolization in rural America can inhibit or has inhibited structural formation toward practices of love. As protostructural aspects of social reality, symbols can mediate both social-structural formation toward healthy, life-giving community and also toward toxic, sinful social structures. In rural American contexts, the symbolization of whiteness and white supremacy can twist the life-giving, love-nurturing aspects of the moral community away from themselves by mediating evils of racism into the fabric of rural social reality. If the moral community is a fundamental mode of rural social self-understanding, the excising of nonwhite members from that self-understanding unjustly narrows the conceptual and ethical scope of the rural moral community, along with its benefits and responsibilities, and white supremacy does exactly that. White supremacy in rural contexts collapses conceptions of who is "local"—and thereby part of the moral community—into the social calculus of whiteness, inhibiting or preventing the full expression of the local moral community with all its members, instead excluding from recognition and solidarity those persons and communities who do not fulfill its racist symbolization.

Beyond racism, symbolic reductionism also curtails the vitality of the rural moral community. Collapsing complex social realities into easily digestible symbolic mediations may make reckoning with one's social context feel like an easier or more efficient endeavor, but this is a fallacious ease. In the complexity of social reality resides the truth—and humanity—of that social reality, and to artificially reduce it by allowing symbols to substitute rather than mediate that reality ultimately leads to a tyranny of social untruth that inhibits the real exercise of love between persons and groups. Similarly, symbolization can also move beyond mere substitution of complex social reality into mediations of untruth itself. Lying symbols can make real in their communities the falsehoods they bear, giving them social weight and potency that lead to harm. All this is to say that while symbolization catalyzes structural formation of social contexts, in rural spaces (as well as others), this catalysis is not necessarily ethically beneficial. Symbols, like many other artifacts of social reality, can mediate sin and untruth just as they can also mediate justice and love.

CHAPTER SIX

Symbolization and Rural Virtual Community

Introduction: Rural Online

In spring 2024, my daughter, who was nine at the time, and I visited an elderly friend of ours to chat and bring her some Easter flowers. In truth, she is primarily my daughter's friend (though she generously puts up with me), having been a welcoming pillar of the church community where we worship since long before our family ever became members. Nearly as soon as my daughter was old enough to hold a conversation, she and this kind woman would chat regularly before and after church—and, often enough, during as well—exploring with vigor and enthusiasm whatever topics bubbled up between them. Our friend had been a kindergarten teacher for decades prior to her retirement and took it as something of a second vocation to extend particular welcome to the young children who visited or regularly attended the church's services. On the morning we stopped by her home, she was resting in her recliner, recovering from a surgery she had had in the weeks prior. There had been some complications, making the recovery slower than expected, and while she maintained a hopeful and even jovial demeanor, she missed being able to attend liturgy in person. Luckily, she told us, the church had never stopped its livestreaming of worship services that had begun early in the COVID-19 pandemic, and while she still wished to be there in person, attending online was a passable substitute, at least for a while. She could still see her friends (though through observation rather than interaction), could worship synchronously with the community, could hear her name and others in the community prayers, and generally could access far more of her faith community's life than would have been possible otherwise. It wasn't the same as being there in person to chat with my daughter, she said, but it also wasn't nothing.

I start with this brief image of one form of virtual religious community—an experience certainly not unique to me or my church—because the challenges thrust on liturgical communities during and in the wake of the COVID-19 pandemic bear a striking resemblance to some of the challenges that have been percolating in rural communities ever since the possibility of virtual/online participation in community has become conceptually and logistically viable. In both cases, a central challenge is what to do when locality—physical proximity in the case of rural communities and physical assembly in the case of liturgical ones—becomes either impossible or perceived as unnecessary. If a community derives its identity in large part from physical locality, of what can that community consist when locality either dissipates or recedes in relevance? Can such a community survive virtual augmentation or substitution, and, if so, in what ways? What can or must change, and of what does the new hybrid or online community consist? In essence, can physical locality—a cornerstone of social architecture in both rural social reality and liturgical ecclesial reality—be safely removed or shifted without damaging the foundations, or do the symbolic structures that rested on that cornerstone buckle and collapse?

To begin addressing the role of symbol and symbolization in mediating the challenges and benefits of online participation in community for rural social reality, this chapter begins by outlining what is at stake for rural social contexts in the proliferation of online life and community. *That* the local is essential for rural social life has been a central point of our discussion thus far, particularly in chapters 1 and 4; what locality *means*, and how symbolizations mediate such meaning, takes on distinct challenges when faced with the massive proliferation of online reality and community life. Having outlined this, the chapter then moves to harvesting some of the fruit of recent liturgical and sacramental theological work, which has been at pains especially since the pandemic to make sense of concepts like presence, participation, assembly, and communion in contexts where physical bodily proximity is prevented or relativized. The fields have thus far not reached a consensus—it might be naive to expect such a thing so quickly—but the treatment of symbol as a central category for making headway in accounting for online ecclesial and liturgical reality is illuminative. Subsequently, the chapter moves to a treatment of symbol and online reality as encountered from a rural contextual perspective, focusing on the modalities and the *stuff* of symbolization and their relationship to rural aesthetics and social self-understandings. The chapter then concludes with a brief exploration of whether and how symbolizations in online space have the capacity to mediate health and vitality of rural social contexts without disintegrating their central distinguishing characteristics.

Rural Contexts and Life Online

Perhaps it is helpful at the outset of this discussion to note that the question of life and community online is not one of *whether* it takes place or whether one or a community should participate in it. Massive swaths of personal and social life—rural and nonrural—take place in virtual space rather than physical space. Access to banking and financial institutions is largely online even if physical access to banks endures, cultural and entertainment resources proliferate in online space, job seeking and acquisition are often mediated at least partially through online resources, health-care providers make significant use of online portals and billing, and even simple knowledge of one's own community (where to find grocery stores, churches, parks, businesses, etc.) can often be the function of a search engine, just to name a few aspects of rural and nonrural life that have increasingly come to rely on mediation through cyberspace.

Some level of online participation in social reality may be nearly universally assumed by many entities in the United States—and certainly it is increasingly viewed as necessary in many sectors—but that does not mean that reliable access to online social reality is universally available. The US Department of Agriculture notes that "22.3 percent of Americans in rural areas and 27.7 percent of Americans in Tribal lands lack coverage from fixed terrestrial 25/3 Mbps broadband, as compared to only 1.5 percent of Americans in urban areas."[1] This disparity is not new, and it has meant that particular ways of living and interacting online have proliferated more slowly in many rural areas than in nonrural ones in the United States. While this has certainly inhibited some level of social participation, supporting those aspects of rural consciousness that feel rural areas tend to be overlooked with regard to accessing necessities and amenities, it has also meant that many rural spaces have had more time—though not by choice—to reckon with the advent of online social reality. Such extra time is not necessarily a blessing or a curse; it is simply an acknowledgment that some ways of adjusting to online mediation of social reality in nonrural spaces are only now emerging in different ways in rural ones.

One of the primary ways online social reality is impacting rural contexts is a massive increase in the efficiency by which nonlocal ideas, concerns, entities, and perspectives can find voice in local rural spaces. It has always been the case that nonlocal factors have interfaced significantly with local rural life,[2] but an essential aspect of rural social self-understanding hinges on participation in and belonging to the local. The rural moral community is a symbolizing concept that works to mediate both personal and social identity for a great many in rural contexts of the United States; the local school and its mascot, the local grocery or hardware store, the local church(es), the local park, the local bar—all of these are more than simply *present* in rural contexts. They *mediate* the presence of a social reality that does not easily admit substitutions. Locality runs deep in rural consciousness, a potent mediation of who a person is in irreducible relation to the rural space a person is from.

---

1. US Department of Agriculture, "E-Connectivity for All Rural Americans Is a Modern-Day Necessity," accessed March 18, 2025, https://www.usda.gov/broadband. See also the Federal Communications Commission, "2020 Broadband Deployment Report," April 24, 2020, https://docs.fcc.gov/public/attachments/FCC-20-50A1.pdf.

2. In this, Conn's work is illuminative (Conn, *The Lies of the Land*).

The very modality of online social reality tends to erode this central piece of what it is to exist as rural. Telecommunication has always carried a certain delocalizing character, but mediation of so much social interaction in and through cyberspace can act as an inhibitor to concern for and even awareness of localized issues, challenges, gifts, and persons. Part of the reason for this is that in many rural social interactions, multiple pertinent social structures overlap in whatever action one takes. Buying groceries is rarely just acquiring food in a rural context; it is also interaction with the cashier who attends high school with your nephew, and a chance meeting with your dentist in the cereal aisle, and a negotiation of parking space with an acquaintance from church, all while participating in the financial life of the local community. All of this is part of making the rural community what it is, not in the abstract but in the concrete and specific context of a particular social reality. Structures of education, business, health care, religion, and government can all inhabit strikingly close or overlapping social space in rural communities. Excising social interaction into online space, then, removes one or more layers of these overlapping structural mediations of social identity. To be clear, this is not always a bad thing. Sometimes, for example, it may be helpful to *not* know one's pharmacist on a personal level when one is picking up a prescription. Like a game of Jenga, however, rural social identity then becomes a game of which supports can be removed from the local and placed in online space, and how many, before the rural social identity cannot support itself and collapses.

There is a certain irony in this. Rural spaces in the United States are often characterized by the long travel distances required simply to exist in them and access necessary goods and services. To this extent, telecommunication and access to online social life should also be a boon for rural social contexts, in that one may be able to live into rural social identity without all the travel time. In some cases, this has been exactly what has happened; for example, in the case of our friend recovering from surgery, she did not tune in to just any online church service—she specifically tuned in to the livestream of her local church. The difficulty appears when symbolization of the social identity changes. When online participation in social reality is perceived to mediate a social reality adequately similar to, or more attractive than, physical social reality, the nonlocalized character of online social reality strikes at the very heart of rural social identity: its locality. The personal relationships with physically proximate neighbors through which the moral community's sense of home and values are mediated either change modality or dissipate altogether. Without social interactions bound to the local, the rural moral community risks disintegration.

Exacerbating this risk is the concomitant perception that if one can choose which parts of social life one can take online, then one may also be able to choose membership in whichever social contexts one can access in cyberspace. To a certain limited extent this is the case—certainly membership in particular online communities is a function of choice and affinity, as well as of algorithms, marketing, and propaganda—but it is *not* the case that rural social reality, mediated through the symbolization of the moral community, can be translated into an online function of free choice and association. The very freedom of association—and dissociation—that conditions online community undercuts the responsibility to and accountability for shared social reality that constitutes the rural moral community. Neighborliness, in the sense of the rural moral community, is not *simply* an affective state that can be crafted by commiseration with the like-minded, nor is its affective component an end in itself. To the extent that neighborliness carries emotional or affective content, such content is, within the framework of the rural moral community, inextricably linked with solidary actions within and on behalf of one's community. In some cases this is possible online, but in many cases it is *inescapable* in rural social reality.

There is an additional way by which online social reality can undercut the rural moral community: the sense of feeling at home, or of belonging. Such affects can be relatively easy to replicate in online space, where communities with the same beliefs, perspectives, biases, affinities, and sensibilities can be both quick and efficient to access. Add to this the algorithmic interest in *making* people feel at home and a sense of belonging in particular online spaces, driven by monetization of both attention and data, and at least from the perspective of affect or emotion, online community can *feel* better than one's physically proximate moral community. Such emotion can quickly be tied not just to feelings of being at home but also of perceptions of the true and the good. If it feels good to be told I'm right and that my perspectives on the world are accurate and worthy, then the vested interest in online platforms and entities to mediate that emotional response will also precipitate moral and cognitive conviction, not just affective satisfaction.

For example, if my hypothetical small-town neighbor Sharon argues with me ceaselessly, but I can find solace in online groups reinforcing my own stances, the resulting entrenchment can fray the fabric of the moral community that *needs both* Sharon and me—not simply as present entities but as active participants whose sense of personal and social identity is bound to belonging to a place and each other. If I have the freedom to choose between being in community with Sharon and being in a community where I am rarely, if ever, challenged, my affective sense of belonging comes into direct competition with the integrity of the local social reality to which I claim to belong. In such cases, finding commonality with distant conversation partners can supersede the complexity of navigating care for physically proximate neighbors with whom I do not see eye to eye. The results can be disastrous for the rural moral community, whose very vitality is tied to belonging to the local.

Moving the Body Online: Insights from Liturgical/Sacramental Theology

In 2020, questions of how to maintain a connection to the local community through nonlocal mediation, and especially cyberspace, became a central focus for church communities who were largely prevented from physically assembling by the COVID-19 pandemic. Particularly for churches whose liturgical traditions hinge on sacramentality, the prevention of bodily assembly presented a significant challenge. Sacramentality, to give a far too brief definition, is a concept centered on encountering the divine through created, bodily means.[3] It is deeply tied to symbolization, in that changing the bodily aspects of a particular sacramental practice (bread, wine, assembly, water, oil, etc.) shifts the mediation itself. Throughout the history of Christianity, this concept, along with others, acted as a kind of guard against Gnosticism and its historical echoes, which tended to dualistically prioritize the spiritual, intellectual, nonbodily aspects of human existence over and against the fleshiness of what it means to be human.[4] Notwithstanding the ever-popular caricature that in Christianity, the spirit matters, while the body doesn't,[5] Christian theology has been at pains to emphasize the importance of bodily presence and mediation nearly since its inception. That Jesus became *bodily* incarnate matters, that he rose *bodily* from the dead matters, and that divine presence continues to be mediated bodily through things like sacramental practice also continues to matter. If Christianity—or Christian liturgical/sacramental practice—were to let go of the importance of bodily presence and mediation, *the* central claim of Christianity, that God became incarnate in a human body, would fall by the wayside, a theologically fatal move.[6]

To be sure, bodily presence is not simply identical with locality, but the two are mutually resonant concepts. To be local is to *have been here*

3. For a more developed discussion of the concept of sacramentality, see Larson-Miller, *Sacramentality Renewed.*

4. See, for example, Matthew John Paul Tan, "Sarah Coakley and the Prayers of the Digital Body of Christ," in *Sarah Coakley and the Future of Systematic Theology*, ed. Janice McRandal (Fortress Press, 2016), 159–186.

5. This is something I (and I suspect a great many other) teachers encounter regularly in introductory theology classes. Whenever I ask the students who grew up exposed to an idea of Christianity that prioritized the spiritual and ignored the bodily, a significant majority of students with experience of Christianity raise their hands. The idea that Christianity might also care about the body is not wholly alien, but it does not rarely land in these contexts as an obvious thing.

6. For an illuminating exploration of this question in relation to technology and artificial intelligence, see Noreen Herzfeld, *The Artifice of Intelligence: Divine and Human Relationship in a Robotic Age* (Fortress, 2023).

and to *be here*, and such being is mediated bodily. Chauvet's identification of the body as arch-symbol is illuminative in this; the primary way locality takes on reality is through mediation of individual and communal bodies. In the Christian sacramental imagination,[7] to be bodily present in a local, physical space is the primary mode of liturgical symbolization; it is the primary way that divine presence and meaning are mediated to the Christian liturgical community.

To convert Christian liturgical mediation to an online modality, then, shifts something fundamental in its symbolization. Because symbolization unfolds bodily, changing how bodies interact (i.e., through virtual reality rather than physically proximate reality) also changes the contours of symbolization and the mediation of social and religious reality. In a traditional in-person liturgical celebration, the geographic location of a person's body matters greatly; it would be nonsensical to say that one "was present" at a liturgical celebration when in fact one's body was elsewhere at the time. If the liturgical celebration is mediated through online means, however, both of these integral factors can be relativized or dispensed with. One can be present from any geographical location with accessible internet, and one can attend according to one's own schedule if the liturgy is made available asynchronously. In both cases, the symbolization of online liturgical celebration renders the localization of bodily presence of little importance.

This is *not* to say, however, that online worship actually lets go of or jettisons bodily presence and mediation. Online social interaction still requires the participation of bodies, and it is still mediated *to* particular individual and communal bodies. Fingers on a keyboard, eyes on a screen, ears in headphones, to say nothing of the bodily mediated cognitive and affective faculties that make online social interaction what it is, are all bodily aspects of online-mediated social reality. Additionally, mediation of social reality through cyberspace precipitates bodily effects that never remain limited to cyberspace. Sinful social interactions like

7. For an explanation of this concept in relation to virtual reality, see Katherine G. Schmidt, *Virtual Communion: Theology of the Internet and the Catholic Sacramental Imagination* (Lexington/Fortress, 2020).

cyberbullying, for example, can mediate physically experienced harms, up to and including bodily self-harm and suicide.[8] Socially beneficial interactions like prayer can also carry bodily benefits, like the edification and support experienced by our friend recovering from surgery when she participated online in her church's prayer life. It would be a mistake to think that online mediation of social reality symbolizes a *false* presence or community. Such social reality is quite real, subject to all the structurization and development that critical realist sociology's morphogenetic cycle describes of non-online social reality.

In this way, dualism, an ever-present problem in Christian theology, presents a two-faced danger to navigating the relationship between online and physically proximate liturgical celebration. On the one hand, assuming that bodily presence does not matter or can be effectively circumvented by online liturgical participation suggests a problematically dualistic opposition between the body and whatever non-bodily human reality is imagined to be participating in online liturgy. On the other hand, casting the distinction between online and physically proximate liturgical celebration in absolute terms buys into a similarly problematic dualism between social reality mediated through locality and social reality mediated through cyberspace.[9] There is untruth in suggesting that bodily presence and the resulting social reality are *identical* online and in locality, and there is also untruth in suggesting that there is *no overlap* between how body and society are mediated online and mediated locally.

Liturgical and sacramental theologians, as well as practical theologians and ministers, remain rather split on whether and in what ways online liturgical practice constitutes a net positive or negative for

8. See, for example, the US Department of Health and Human Services, National Institutes of Health, "Cyberbullying Linked with Suicidal Thoughts and Attempts in Young Adolescents," July 12, 2022, https://www.nih.gov/news-events/nih-research-matters/cyberbullying-linked-suicidal-thoughts-attempts-young-adolescents.

9. Sometimes this dualism is quite explicit. See, for example, Casey T. Sigmon, "Failure to Discern the Online/Hybrid Body: A Captivity of the Eucharist," *Currents in Theology and Mission* 50, no. 1 (2023): 14. See also Anna Case-Winters, *Reconstructing a Christian Theology of Nature* (Ashgate, 2007), 24, 69.

Christian religious practice. On the one hand, it stands in and adds to a long line of liturgical practices aimed at facilitating religious participation with those for whom physically proximate worship is either impossible or inadvisable (e.g., bringing communion to those who are sick or homebound). Attending church online while recovering from surgery is one example, but other examples abound. As Jan Schnell points out, "Many people cannot be at in-building worship; immunocompromised health, contagious stages of illness, a family member dealing with autism, and more are all real things that make being in-building impossible. In these instances, getting to be in-building is not about choice or convenience."[10] Additionally, such online participation transcends mere observation. Whereas in the eyes of some, the nearest analog for online liturgical practice is other telecommunication modalities like television and radio, for many who participate in liturgy online, the nearest analog is actually the physically proximate celebration of liturgy itself. Schnell continues, "For those who cannot come to the building, peace, healing, music, and worship of God does occur online. The assembly, both in-building and online, can be gathered together in place. The locally gathered assembly now contains physical bodies in-building and physical bodies online."[11]

Other theologians and ministers remain quite skeptical of the role appropriate for online-mediated liturgical practice in relation to the normative practice of physically proximate liturgy. For some, the problem is primarily theological, in the key of challenging the body's central role in Christian understandings of social reality and redemption (even prior to the pandemic, thinkers like Matthew Tan opined that online prayer "expunges" concern for the body's role in salvation).[12] For others, however, the problem is also social-ethical, in that online social reality's

10. Jan Schnell, "What Constitutes the Gathered Eucharistic Assembly?" *Currents in Theology and Mission* 50, no. 1 (2023): 44.

11. Schnell, "What Constitutes the Gathered Eucharistic Assembly?," 44. Emphasis removed.

12. Tan, "Sarah Coakley and the Prayers of the Digital Body of Christ," 162.

efficiency in facilitating consumer spending and commodification of goods and ideas injects a social toxicity into online liturgy that compromises its symbolization and mediation. Lizette Larson-Miller clarifies these terms, explaining that "at the heart of understanding consumerism and commodification are two essential dimensions: consumption as a primary means of establishing social and personal identity, and fragmentation, both of which impact ritual praxis and sacramental theology in profound ways."[13]

Larson-Miller's insight points to the fact that Christian liturgical practice, at its heart, does not operate according to a logic of market exchange. Liturgical social and religious interactions resist the norms of value calculation that claim to assign a price to all that is. Instead, Christian ritual is a realm of symbolic exchange, outside the calculus of value, in which the stuff of the exchange is primarily the active subjects involved (God, the community, and the persons who make it up), *in and through* the mediation of liturgical symbols. Such symbolization is, on the whole, a practice of gift-giving and gift-receiving in which the primary purposes are less about personal enrichment and much more about relational and religious experience and development.

Such experience and development *can* be mediated online, but a massive share of online space is dominated by commercial endeavors, as well as the data harvesting, retaining, selling, and buying that sustain them. In a word, cyberspace is largely a marketplace (not just of goods and services but also of political opinions, social biases, and ideas both virtuous and vicious), with relatively few exceptions. Part of what distinguishes online social reality from physically local social reality in this view, then, is that the logic of market exchange is built into the very fabric of online existence, a mediation that is inseparable from the particular symbolizations that unfold. Any social entity that resists reducing itself to market exchange and commodification, then (such as

---

13. Lizette Larson-Miller, "Reality of Presence in Virtually Mediated Sacramentality: Has Sacramental Theology Sustained Us?" *Anglican Theological Review* 104, no. 1 (2022): 46.

Christian liturgy or rural moral community), will have a very difficult time doing so in an online modality.

While this is largely the case, it is also important to note that to the extent to which cyberspace is overwhelmingly the domain of market exchange, it is not necessarily that different from many physically local social contexts. Physical social spaces in which one is not expected or encouraged to spend money and consume goods or services can be quite rare, especially in the United States, and there is little to suggest that such spaces show much promise of becoming more common. The operative logic of symbolization then (that of gift exchange) is under threat not just in online social reality but in physically proximate social reality. Such a shared challenge is not just one of subject; it is also a nexus point between the experience of ecclesial social reality (online and not) and rural social reality (online and not). What can be both a blessing and burden for church communities in this sense can likewise be a blessing and burden for rural social contexts.

Symbol, Online Community, and Rural Social Reality

Mediation of rural social reality, like that of ecclesial reality in the context of the COVID-19 pandemic, takes place both through physically proximate modes and through virtual space. Some of the social content exchanged through these distinct modalities can be effectively transposed between them; acquiring car insurance can take place online or in person, networks of delivery systems have made online purchasing of goods efficient alongside in-person shopping, and a whole host of other social interactions can unfold in physically proximate space or in cyberspace according to the preferences and needs of those involved. Only some aspects of social reality can be transposed between online and physical space, however; to the extent that social interactions participate not just in the language pole of signification (that of instrumentalization and market exchange) but also in symbolization (the pole of gift and non-value), their symbolized mediation is not as easily substituted one for the other.

In symbolic exchange—a social interaction within which *what* is exchanged is less important than *who* or *how*—individuals and communities negotiate social space and structure based on the presence, identity, and encounters of the exchange. Such aspects can only analogously be thought of as participating in market exchange and instrumentalization without risking dehumanizing those involved; one does not "purchase" identity, for example. The alternative is their mediation through non-value, through gift-giving. In this way, the modality of the interaction makes all the difference. Consider a hypothetical case in which someone needs help with childcare—perhaps the usual provider is sick or occupied with some other emergent issue. There is a real mediation of care if someone sends an email or social media message of support and even more so if such a message also includes online mediation of financial support for the childcare, but in both cases, the care remains, to a certain degree, disembodied. Neither expression of care moves directly to addressing the need because the actual practice of childcare cannot be mediated virtually.

On the other hand, if a physically proximate person reaches out with a message of care and support, that person may also be able to provide the needed childcare itself. In doing so, the set of social relationships shifts from "caring neighbors" to "neighbors willing and able to help" in the ways most pressing in the situation. Put differently, in the case of needing childcare, the physically proximate neighbor has access to a mediation of service that the online neighbor does not. Providing such service is *more* than providing service; it symbolizes (mediates) the presence of both (1) particular neighbors who are willing to help and (2) a community that has fostered relationships within which mutual support is possible and encouraged. This is part of what makes the rural moral community what it is. The feelings of being at home and doing the right things are not constituted out of thin air; they require symbolization by physically embodied reality in order to become socially identifiable and determinative. Only when they take on flesh does the rural moral community become something more than a pleasant imaginary idea.

This nontransposability of symbolization between cyberspace and physically proximate community becomes more pronounced when divisive issues and polarization (political, social, religious, or otherwise) raise questions of where the boundaries lie in the rural moral community and in what ways those boundaries are mediated. A primary operative characteristic of rural moral community is neighborliness that is occasioned (demanded?) by proximity. For many rural communities to function well, this primacy of proximity is an essential part of what holds the fabric of the community together. While it is relatively common for rural folks also to cite shared values and perspectives as indicative of their moral community, it is the living out of life in physically proximate space—and the conviction that doing so is a *good* thing, which requires work and investment—that provides the groundwork for shared community vitality even when values and perspectives are *not* shared.

Polarized and polarizing ideas find efficient dissemination through online media. This is not itself a bad thing—unifying and upbuilding messages find the same efficient dissemination—but it can have a sizable impact on the social imagination of particular rural communities and the rural in general. By *imagination*, I do not mean a kind of fiction-fabricating faculty; rather, the social imaginary of rural communities interfaces with rural aesthetics to construct the self-understanding of what rural social existence is. The complicating factor that comes with online augmentation of rural social reality is that images disconnected from rural existence can become normative aesthetic expressions of the rural if they are given sufficient rural and nonrural weight. A rural mythology tied to both rural and nonrural imaginaries is not novel with the advent of social reality in cyberspace. As Conn notes, Theodore Roosevelt's affinity with the rural, even that mediated by governmental structures, was conditioned as much by his own imagination of rural reality as it was by any lived experience of rural reality.[14] The benefits to rural social space precipitated by the New Deal and its aftereffects were

14. Conn, *The Lies of the Land*, 87–88.

likewise influenced by Franklin Roosevelt's affection for small-town life but filtered through nonrural initiatives in Washington, DC.[15]

What online mediation of social imagination brings with it that *is* novel is the speed and impact it provides for such imagination. Images, videos, audios, and various kinds of discourse can be nearly instantly and globally accessible, playing on the social imaginaries of anyone whose attention they can grab. This again transmits the mediation of social reality from the realm of non-value back into market exchange with staggering force. What it is to speak effectively in online space is often concomitant with what it is to speak so that people *pay attention*, and that attention can be both monetized and instrumentalized for particular social, economic, and political aims. For example, when country music artist Jason Aldean released his now infamous song "Try That in a Small Town" in 2023, its impact was nearly immediate and significantly polarized. The song, which paints a picture of small-town vigilante justice as effectively how rural social order is kept, as opposed to the song's postulating of big-city permissiveness that is implied to cause civil unrest and unsafety, was adopted as a kind of anthem for many who were drawn to the idea of rural neighborliness connoting a violent protection from perceived outside agitators. For others, the song (and its music video, which featured sequences of news footage taken from Black Lives Matter protests and other events)[16] mediated racist and xenophobic tropes that dressed up bigotry in the trappings of small-town values.

While Aldean himself grew up in Macon, Georgia (population roughly 153,000), and resides in Nashville (population roughly 700,000),[17] his small-town violence aesthetic struck a chord with both

15. Conn, *The Lies of the Land*, 89–90.

16. Chris Willman, "Jason Aldean's 'Try That in a Small Town' Video Undergoes Edits, Loses Footage of BLM Protests Used Without Permission," *Variety*, July 26, 2023, https://variety.com/2023/music/news/jason-aldean-video-edited-blm-footage-try-that-small-town-1235680869/.

17. Arwa Mahdawi, "Jason Aldean's 'Try That in a Small Town' Sums Up the Delusions of the Right Wing," *Guardian*, July 20, 2023, https://www.theguardian.com/commentisfree/2023/jul/20/jason-aldean-try-that-in-a-small-town-rightwing-embrace.

rural and nonrural residents of the United States in significantly disparate ways—though the differences did not necessarily map easily onto the cliché rural-nonrural divide. The symbolization of the song mediated an image of the small town whose identity as a moral community is predicated on its violent enforcement of one perspective at the expense of others seen as nonlocal and therefore unwelcome. It blithely misses the point that the rural moral community *itself* contains diverse perspectives, held in community by the very adherence to local life that the song weaponizes. Such weaponization cuts the rural moral community to the quick, twisting it from a home for those who live there into an imagined barracks of ideological purity. The danger to rural social fabric is not simply in the song itself, though there is some there too; the danger is also in the online proliferation of its message, mediating an image of social reality that is toxic to the very social reality it struggles to symbolize.

The fix to this—if one is possible—cannot be a retreat from online social reality. Indeed, there may be no fix in the proper sense of the term. Instead, rural social reality is maturing in its accommodation and use of cyberspace to mediate social life, not unlike religious communities in the wake of the pandemic. For example, in agricultural enterprise, this is nearly self-evident given a quick glance; access to the vast expanse of economic, ecological, and other data that comes with online connection has quickly become a default tool in understanding, planning, and revising farm enterprises. In a more civic-oriented example, many small cities and townships have begun to livestream their city council meetings or township board meetings, facilitating both transparency and local participation that would be far less feasible otherwise. Similar examples abound; what cyberspace symbolizes with regard to social reality tends to be both efficient and accessible, but it can grate directly against the operative logic of symbolization—that of gift and non-value. Rural life itself *is* a gift, and it resists reduction to instrumentalization and the monetization of market exchange. It is symbolized—mediated—by the modalities that constitute it: local life, lived as shared by those who call the place home, and in which that shared life unfolds in celebration, grief, perseverance, and all that conditions a community in the truest sense. Symbolization of rural social reality takes on flesh in those who live it, and it is in their shared lives and experiences that the truth of rural social reality can be best encountered.

Conclusion

This chapter has largely argued that while online mediation of certain aspects of social reality is inescapable and even beneficial, the necessity of locality in rural social self-understanding means that transposition of in-person social interaction to online-mediated social interaction carries a risk of eroding the vitality of rural moral community. Put succinctly, irreducibly bodily aspects of human life—eating, drinking, shelter, childcare, and myriad others—remain anchored in the not online, fleshy world of social interaction and are symbolized therein as well. In a healthy rural moral community, these and other aspects of human social life unfold as mediatory of social identity—of home and who a person is in the community. To the degree that social interactions are moved uncritically to the delocalized context of cyberspace, the social realities that rely on locality in order to function well tend to be hollowed out, becoming socially brittle or fragile and risking collapse. Such weakening does not need to be the case, however, if online social reality can be carefully leveraged to support rather than erode rural social vitality. Doing so tends to take the form of mediating connections that can be difficult otherwise—due to travel time, inclement weather, health concerns, or any number of other factors—but in rural contexts, this mediation must hold the importance of the local at its center.

Put differently, online mediation of social reality is not necessarily a threat to rural social vitality unless the delocalized character of online reality supplants the localized commitments of the rural moral community. Such risks can look like exporting one's social identity (i.e., rejecting one's local social home in favor of more nonlocal interests, concerns, and ideologies), or importing ideologies and propaganda that aim to instrumentalize rather than vitalize one's home community, or similar actions of dissolving locality. If a community and the persons in it can avoid these and similar traps, instead maintaining and regenerating the local nature of the rural moral community through both online and on-the-ground ways, there is little necessary danger of online reality inhibiting rural vitality. Some rural churches have discovered this well, fostering both their in-the-building ministry and online connections to order them toward healthy and efficient ministerial care for their rural contexts.

In the final account, cyberspace does mediate significant portions of social reality, inclusive of many of the symbols that operate in particular contexts. While overreliance on online mediation may threaten to flatten or caricaturize those contexts, from a rural perspective at least, there remains significant potential for healthy mediation and symbolization through online means, if the anchor of locality remains in the rural moral community.

EPILOGUE

When I make the drive out to our family's farm in west-central Minnesota, there is a marked difference between the way traffic interacts on the two-lane paved county roads and state highways, on the one hand, and the way it interacts on the gravel roads that comprise the final miles before my destination, on the other. On the paved roads, interactions with other vehicles and the persons in them are largely limited to simply observing normal traffic laws. The horizon of awareness regarding other traffic is populated essentially by knowing which other vehicles are on the road, not necessarily who is driving them, and still less by what relationship one might have to them. Once I'm driving on the gravel roads, however, many drivers don't see *just* other vehicles. They see the persons *in* those vehicles, the directions they're driving in relation to local landmarks and likely destinations, and often engage in a brief social calculus regarding their relationship to other drivers.

When I meet another vehicle driving the relatively slow speeds that the gravel roads near the farm require, the other driver and I very often make eye contact. Then, depending on our familiarity or lack thereof, we often exchange some kind of gesture of acknowledgment (a wave, a nod of the head, or just the raising of a few fingers or hand off the steering wheel in greeting). Such gestures of acknowledgment do not necessarily carry some kind of deep meaning, but they participate in a system of symbols within which public acknowledgment and familiarity go hand in hand in determining the functioning of a local community. The presence or absence of a wave, as well as the presence of a particular kind of vehicle on a certain road (Car? Van? SUV? Milk truck? The elder Durheims' pickup?), occasion a brief inner monologue of "Do I know that person? How, or in what context? If I don't know them, are they headed in a direction or on a road with a likely destination I know well? Maybe they're connected with a local family or institution?" and other such questions. More than once I've waved at another hitherto unfamiliar driver and watched them crane their neck in an effort to keep looking at who waved to them after I pass, only to see them on another occasion and have them return the greeting this second time around. Even if we've never met, the symbolization in exchanging gestures of greeting between drivers is part of the symbolic order of that rural space. It's a small building block of the community feel and aesthetic, but it is a building block just the same.

My point is this: A person does not choose the meanings of symbols on their own authority or according to their own whim. For that matter, communities themselves rarely have deterministic control over the mediation of symbols in their midst. Rather, persons enter into worlds of symbolized meaning through shared interaction, and both presence and absence, action and inaction, serve to speak social relation and structures into existence. I wouldn't *have* to make eye contact with other drivers on the gravel roads near the farm, but my choice not to do so would nevertheless mediate a social meaning. A relatively surface-level example like this is generally fairly inconsequential, but there is a literacy of the symbolic order at work in seeing where this example finds its roots. There is more than gesture and greeting; there is mediation of presence and absence in the social interaction. If that mediation is multiplied by being shared among many persons or accepted as a common (read: expected) way of doing things in a social context, the small interactions can become quite large or at least illuminative of how the symbolic order functions there. Whenever I've shared Yackel-Juleen's story of the farmer vomiting after beginning to plow up his fields with someone who is steeped in the practice of farming, the response has never been surprise. It is a legible and even anticipated—if unwelcome—part of the story because within the overlapping systems of symbols that make up rural agrarian life in their experiences, how could it not be? It is something of a given—apt in the logic of symbolic exchange—a mediation of an aspect of what it is to live as part of a rural, agrarian context. Nobody actively chose that mediation or meaning, but it remains real—given—nonetheless.

My hope is that attending to literacy with regard to the multiplication and multivalence of symbolizations in social reality can produce approaches to social ethics and ministry that misfire far less frequently. Attending to symbolization, wherein we receive each other's presence as a gift rather than approach each other as disinterested founts of information, is a practice ordered toward humanizing each other—including those with whom we do not see eye to eye—and navigating social space in such a way that we might more easily practice the work of love. Certainly not everyone may have this goal, but from a Christian theological perspective, anything less risks unmooring from the anchor of what it is to live together on the way to God's reign. This work is in no way limited to rural spaces or contexts; symbols do their social work and bear their social weight in contexts far beyond the fields, mines, forests, factories, and small-town main streets of rural America. Rural life is dear to me and has given me who I am, so I have begun there, but reckoning with the social depth of symbolization is an expansive aim. My hope is that doing so can lead more easily to social practices of love, and my prayer is that we in the United States have a shared wherewithal to do so, in both our rural spaces and our nonrural ones. May we accompany one another and attend to one another, each in our own language.

BIBLIOGRAPHY

Albrecht, Don E. *Building a Resilient Twenty-First-Century Economy for Rural America*. University Press of Colorado, 2020.

Albrecht, Don E. "Donald Trump and Changing Rural/Urban Voting Patterns." *Journal of Rural Studies* 91 (2022): 148–156. https://doi.org/10.1016/j.jrurstud.2022.03.009.

American Health Care Association / National Center for Assisted Living. "ICYMI: Democrat Lawmaker Opposition of Federal Staffing Mandate for Nursing Homes Is Growing." November 30, 2023. https://www.ahcancal.org/News-and-Communications/Press-Releases/Pages/ICYMI-Democrat-Lawmaker-Opposition-Of-Federal-Staffing-Mandate-For-Nursing-Homes-Is-Growing.aspx#:~:text=Much%20of%20the%20opposition%20comes,with%20this%20impossible%2C%20unfunded%20mandate.

Archer, Margaret, Roy Bhaskar, Andrew Collier, Tony Lawson, and Alan Norrie, eds. *Critical Realism: Essential Readings*. Routledge, 1998.

Archer, Margaret S. *Being Human: The Problem of Agency*. Cambridge University, 2000.

Archer, Margaret S. *Culture and Agency: The Place of Culture in Social Theory*. Cambridge University, 1996.

Archer, Margaret S. *Realist Social Theory: The Morphogenetic Approach*. Cambridge University, 1995.

Artz, Georgeanne. "Rural Area Brain Drain: Is It a Reality?" *Choices: A Publication of the American Agricultural Economics Association* (2003): 11–15.

Ashwood, Loka. *For-Profit Democracy: Why the Government Is Losing the Trust of Rural America*. Yale University, 2018.

Associated Press. "CSB, SJU Investigate Alleged Sex Competition." *KNSI News*, October 20, 2021. https://knsiradio.com/2021/10/20/csb-sju-investigate-alleged-sex-competition/.

Associated Press. "What Is 'Ordo Amoris?' Vice President JD Vance Invokes This Medieval Catholic Concept." Associated Press, February 6, 2025. https://apnews.com/article/jd-vance-catholic-theology-migration-e868af574fb2e742c6ed3d756c569769.

Babka, Susie Paulik. *Through the Dark Field: The Incarnation Through an Aesthetics of Vulnerability*. Liturgical Press, 2017.

Badger, Emily. "As American as Apple Pie? The Rural Vote's Disproportionate Slice of Power." *New York Times*, November 20, 2016. https://www.nytimes.com/2016/11/21/upshot/as-american-as-apple-pie-the-rural-votes-disproportionate-slice-of-power.html.

Barlett, Peggy F. *American Dreams, Rural Realities: Family Farms in Crisis*. University of North Carolina, 1993.

Beaton, Rhodora E. *Embodied Words, Spoken Signs: Sacramentality and the Word in Rahner and Chauvet*. Fortress, 2014.

Beck, Michael Adam, and Tyler Kleeberger. *Fresh Expressions of the Rural Church*. Abingdon, 2022.

Belcher, Kimberly Hope. *Efficacious Engagement: Sacramental Participation in the Trinitarian Mystery*. Liturgical Press, 2011.

Bell, Catherine. *Ritual: Perspectives and Dimensions*. Oxford University, 1997.

Bell, Catherine. *Ritual Theory, Ritual Practice*. Oxford University, 2009.

Benzow, August. "Rural America Is Not All Trump Country: A Closer Look at the Rural Counties That Biden Won." *Economic Innovation Group*, November 17, 2020. https://eig.org/rural-america-is-not-all-trump-country/.

Berg, Jenny, Stephanie Dickrell, and David Unze. "Sex Trafficking: The Victims Next Door." *SC Times*, July 21, 2016. https://www.sctimes.com/story/news/local/2016/07/21/sex-trafficking-victims-next-door/87248556/.

Bevans, Stephen B. *Models of Contextual Theology*. Orbis, 2009.

Bhaskar, Roy. *A Realist Theory of Science*. Routledge, 2008.

Bishops' Committee on the Liturgy. *Environment and Art in Catholic Worship*. US Catholic Conference, 1978.

Bonilla-Silva, Eduardo. *Racism Without Racists: Color-Blind Racism and the Persistence of Racial Inequality in America*. 6th ed. Rowman and Littlefield, 2022.

Bourdeyne, Philippe, and Bruce T. Morrill, eds. *Sacraments: Revelation of the Humanity of God*. Liturgical Press, 2008.

Bourdieu, Pierre. *Outline of a Theory of Practice*. Cambridge University, 1977.

Brookie, Drew. "Rural Veterans and the Tyranny of Distance." US Department of Agriculture, 2011. https://www.usda.gov/media/blog/2011/08/03/rural-veterans-and-tyranny-distance.

Brunk, Timothy. *The Sacraments and Consumer Culture*. Liturgical Press, 2020.

Capps, Randy, and Michael Fix. "Changing the Playbook: Immigrants and the COVID-19 Response in Two U.S. Communities." Migration Policy Institute, July 2022. https://www.migrationpolicy.org/sites/default/files/publications/mpi_covid19-immigrant-communities_final.pdf.

Caputo, John D., and Michael J. Scanlon, eds. *God, the Gift, and Postmodernism*. Indiana University, 1999.

Carr, Patrick J., and Maria J. Kefalas. *Hollowing Out the Middle: The Rural Brain Drain and What It Means for America*. Beacon, 2009.

Case-Winters, Anna. *Reconstructing a Christian Theology of Nature*. Ashgate, 2007.

Cavadini, John C., and Donald Wallenfang, eds. *Pope Francis and the Event of Encounter*. Pickwick, 2018.

Cavanaugh, William. *Torture and Eucharist: Theology, Politics, and the Body of Christ*. Blackwell, 1998.

Certeau, Michel de. *The Practice of Everyday Life*. University of California, 1988.

Chauvet, Louis-Marie. "The Liturgy in Its Symbolic Space." In *Liturgy and the Body*, edited by Louis-Marie Chauvet and Francois Kabasele Lumbala. Orbis, 1995.

Chauvet, Louis-Marie. *Symbol and Sacrament: A Sacramental Reinterpretation of Christian Existence*. Liturgical Press, 1995.

Chauvet, Louis-Marie. *The Sacraments: Word of God at the Mercy of the Body*. Liturgical Press, 2001.

Chupungco, Anscar J. *What, Then, Is Liturgy?* Liturgical Press, 2010.

Cloutier, David. "Sociological Self-Knowledge, Critical Realism, and Christian Ethics." *Studies in Christian Ethics* 34, no. 2 (2021): 158–170.

Cones, Bryan. *This Assembly of Believers: The Gifts of Difference in the Church at Prayer*. SCM Press, 2020.

Conn, Stephen. *The Lies of the Land: Seeing Rural America for What It Is—and Isn't*. University of Chicago, 2023.

Cooper, Ryan. "Elon Musk and the Decline of Tesla." *American Prospect*, June 17, 2024. https://prospect.org/power/2024-06-17-elon-musk-decline-of-tesla/#:~:text=dealerships%20this%20year.-,In%20the%20first%20quarter%20of%20this%20year%2C%20Tesla%20sales%20slumped,namely%20affluent%2C%20environmentally%20conscious%20liberals.

Copeland, M. Shawn. *Enfleshing Freedom: Body, Race, and Being*. Fortress, 2010.

Crainshaw, Jill Y. *When I in Awesome Wonder: Liturgy Distilled from Daily Life*. Liturgical Press, 2017.

Cramer, Katherine J. *The Politics of Resentment: Rural Consciousness in Wisconsin and the Rise of Scott Walker*. University of Chicago, 2016.

Cramer Walsh, Katherine. "Putting Inequality in Its Place: Rural Consciousness and the Power of Perspective." *American Political Science Review* 106, no. 3 (2012): 517–532.

Daly, Daniel J. *The Structures of Virtue and Vice.* Georgetown University, 2021.

Derrida, Jacques. *Given Time: I. Counterfeit Money.* Translated by Peggy Kamuf. University of Chicago, 1994.

Derrida, Jacques. *The Gift of Death.* Translated by David Wills. University of Chicago, 1996.

Dudley, Kathryn Marie. *Debt and Dispossession: Farm Loss in America's Heartland.* University of Chicago, 2000.

Duncan, Cynthia M. *Worlds Apart: Poverty and Politics in Rural America.* 2nd ed. Yale University, 2014.

Duneier, Mitchell. *Sidewalk.* Farrar, Straus, and Giroux, 2020.

Durheim, Benjamin. "Anger and Hope in Rural American Liturgy." *Religions* 13 (2022): 590. https://doi.org/10.3390/rel13070590.

Durheim, Benjamin. "Converting Consumerism: A Liturgical-Ethical Application of Critical Realism." *Religions* 10, no. 5 (May 2019): 1–13.

Durheim, Benjamin. "Country Heaven: Toward a Rural Aesthetic of Salvation." Paper presented at the 78th Annual Convention of the Catholic Theological Society of America. Baltimore, MD, June 2024.

Durheim, Benjamin. "Epicletic Advance? Viewing Eucharistic Fellowship Through Critical Realism and the Epiclesis." *Proceedings of the North American Academy of Liturgy* 2020 (2020): 87–101.

Durheim, Benjamin. "Just Liturgy: Connecting Theological Ethics and Liturgical Practice." *Proceedings of the North American Academy of Liturgy* 2018 (2018): 79–93.

Enger, John. "Anti-Islam Speakers Urge Rural MN Crowds to Prepare for Muslim Attack." *MPRNews*, October 25, 2016. https://www.mprnews.org/story/2016/10/25/antiislam-speakers-urge-rural-mn-prepare-muslim-attack.

Farley, Margaret. *Just Love: A Framework for Christian Sexual Ethics.* Continuum, 2006.

Favazza, Joseph. "The Efficacy of Ritual Resistance: The Case of Catholic Sacramental Reconciliation." *Worship* 72, no. 3 (1998): 210–220.

Federal Communications Commission. "2020 Broadband Deployment Report." April 24, 2020. https://docs.fcc.gov/public/attachments/FCC-20-50A1.pdf.

Fields, Stephen M. *Being as Symbol: On the Origins and Development of Karl Rahner's Metaphysics.* Georgetown University, 2000.

Finn, Daniel K. "What Is a Sinful Social Structure?" *Theological Studies* 77, no. 1 (2016): 136–164.

Finn, Daniel K., ed. "Social Structures." In *Moral Agency Within Social Structures and Culture: A Primer on Critical Realism for Christian Ethics.* Georgetown University, 2020.

Finn, Daniel K., ed. "What Is Critical Realism?" In *Moral Agency Within Social Structures and Culture: A Primer on Critical Realism for Christian Ethics.* Georgetown University, 2020.

Finn, Daniel K., ed., *Moral Agency Within Social Structures and Culture: A Primer on Critical Realism for Christian Ethics.* Georgetown University, 2020.

Fitzgerald, Deborah. *Every Farm a Factory: The Industrial Ideal in American Agriculture.* Yale University, 2003.

Flores, Nichole M. *The Aesthetics of Solidarity: Our Lady of Guadalupe and American Democracy.* Georgetown University, 2021.

García-Rivera, Alejandro. *A Wounded Innocence: Sketches for a Theology of Art.* Liturgical Press, 2003.

García-Rivera, Alejandro. *The Community of the Beautiful: A Theological Aesthetics.* Liturgical Press, 1999.

Gerhards, Albert, and Benedikt Kranemann. *Introduction to the Study of Liturgy.* Liturgical Press, 2017.

Gilbert, Jess. *Planning Democracy: Agrarian Intellectuals and the Intended New Deal.* Yale University, 2016.

Gimpel, James G., Nathan Lovin, Bryant Moy, and Andrew Reeves. "The Urban-Rural Gulf in American Political Behavior." *Political Behavior* 42 (2020): 1343–1368. https://doi.org/10.1007/s11109-020-09601-w.

Grady-Hunt, Ayanna. "Larcenia Floyd and Representations of the Divine: The Path to Justice Is Black, Feminine, and Interfaith." *Berkeley Journal of Religion and Theology* 6, no. 1 (2020): 4–9.

Grimes, Katie Walker. *Christ Divided: Antiblackness as Corporate Vice.* Fortress, 2017.

Hagen, Lisa. "Christian Nationalism's Support Is Strongest in Rural, Conservative States." *NPR*, February 28, 2024. https://www.npr.org/2024/02/28/1234304058/christian-nationalism-survey.

Haight, Roger. *Jesus Symbol of God.* Orbis, 2000.

Hall, Kevin. "West Words Had It Right, Not Wrong." *Morrison County Record*, June 19, 2020. https://www.hometownsource.com/morrison_county_record/west-words-had-it-right-not-wrong/article_96dc06d4-b28b-11ea-8483-8706486dec96.html.

Harms, Ernst. "The Rural Consciousness." *Social Forces* 19, no. 1 (1940): 29–40.

Heidegger, Martin. *Identity and Difference.* Translated by Joan Stambaugh. University of Chicago, 2002.

Heidegger, Martin. "Letter on 'Humanism.'" In *Martin Heidegger: Pathmarks*, edited by William McNeill. Cambridge University, 1998.

Herzfeld, Noreen. *The Artifice of Intelligence: Divine and Human Relationship in a Robotic Age*. Fortress, 2023.

Hill Fletcher, Jeannine. *The Sin of White Supremacy: Christianity, Racism, and Religious Diversity in America*. Orbis, 2017.

Hochschild, Arlie Russell. *Strangers in Their Own Land: Anger and Mourning on the American Right*. The New Press, 2016.

Hollenbach, David. *The Common Good and Christian Ethics*. Cambridge University, 2002.

Immerwahr, Daniel. "Beyond the Myth of Rural America." *New Yorker*, October 16, 2023. https://www.newyorker.com/magazine/2023/10/23/beyond-the-myth-of-rural-america.

Isasi-Díaz, Ada María. *La Lucha Continues: Mujerista Theology*. Orbis, 2004.

Jacobs, Nicholas F., and Daniel Shea. *The Rural Voter: The Politics of Place and the Disuniting of America*. Columbia University, 2023.

Jaycox, Michael P. "The Civic Virtues of Social Anger: A Critically Reconstructed Normative Ethic for Public Life." *Journal of the Society of Christian Ethics* 36, no. 1 (2016): 123–143.

Jennings, Willie James. *The Christian Imagination: Theology and the Origins of Race*. Yale University, 2010.

Johnson, Jeff. "'On the Road' Masses Are a Mingling of Creativity and the Holy Spirit." *Central Minnesota Catholic*, June 14, 2023. https://thecentralminnesotacatholic.org/on-the-road-masses-are-a-mingling-of-creativity-and-the-holy-spirit/.

Jones Medine, Carolyn M. "Womanist Spirit and Womanist Healing for Sandra Bland and George Floyd." *Black Women and Religious Cultures* 1, no. 1 (2020): 89–107.

Kammer, Jerry. "The 2006 Swift Raids: Assessing the Impact of Immigration Enforcement Actions at Six Facilities." Center for Immigration Studies, March 18, 2009. https://cis.org/Report/2006-Swift-Raids.

Karst, Layla. "Caught in the Act: Karl Rahner, Brian Flanagan, and the Problem of Liturgical Failure." *Horizons* 50, no. 1 (2023): 32–61.

Katongole, Emmanuel. "'A Blood Thicker than the Blood of Tribalism': Eucharist and Identity in African Politics." *Modern Theology* 30, no. 2 (2014): 319–325.

Kavanaugh, Aiden. *On Liturgical Theology*. Liturgical Press, 1984.

Keenan, James F. *A History of Catholic Theological Ethics*. Paulist, 2022.

Kiel, Micah D. *Apocalyptic Ecology: The Book of Revelation, Earth, and the Future*. Liturgical Press, 2017.

Klimoski, Victor, and Lance Barker, eds. *Abundant Harvest: Essays on Rural Life and Ministry in Honor of Dean and Elsie Freudenberger*. Minnesota Consortium of Theological Schools, 2000.

Larson-Miller, Lizette. "Reality of Presence in Virtually Mediated Sacramentality: Has Sacramental Theology Sustained Us?" *Anglican Theological Review* 104, no. 1 (2022): 37–53.

Larson-Miller, Lizette. *Sacramentality Renewed: Contemporary Conversations in Sacramental Theology*. Liturgical Press, 2016.

Laurance, John D. "Catherine Bell and Liturgical Theology." *Antiphon* 4, no. 2 (1999): 14–18.

Levinas, Emmanuel. *Totality and Infinity: An Essay on Exteriority*. Translated by Alphonso Lingus. Kluwer Academic, 1991.

"Liturgy in Rural Settings." Special Issue. *Liturgy* 32, no. 4 (2017).

Love, Hannah, and Tracy Hadden Loh. "The 'Rural-Urban Divide' Furthers Myths About Race and Poverty—Concealing Effective Policy Solutions." Brookings Institution, December 8, 2020. https://www.brookings.edu/blog/the-avenue/2020/12/08/the-rural-urban-divide-furthers-myths-about-race-and-poverty-concealing-effective-policy-solutions/.

MacGregor, Lyn C. *Habits of the Heartland: Small-Town Life in Modern America*. Cornell, 2010.

Maes, Marieke. "Paul Ricœr: Symbols of Good and Evil in History, the Bible, and in Our Time." *European Journal for Philosophy of Religion* 12, no. 4 (2020): 161–174.

Mahdawi, Arwa. "Jason Aldean's 'Try That in a Small Town' Sums Up the Delusions of the Right Wing." *Guardian*, July 20, 2023. https://www.theguardian.com/commentisfree/2023/jul/20/jason-aldean-try-that-in-a-small-town-rightwing-embrace.

Marion, Jean-Luc. *Being Given: Toward a Phenomenology of Givenness*. Stanford University, 2002.

Massingale, Bryan. *Racial Justice and the Catholic Church*. Orbis, 2010.

McKinney, Matt. "Anti-Muslim Speaking Circuit Runs Through Rural Minnesota." *Star Tribune*, April 17, 2016. https://www.startribune.com/anti-muslim-speaking-circuit-runs-through-rural-minnesota/375924701.

Michel, Virgil. *Christian Social Reconstruction*. Bruce Publishing, 1937.

Minnesota Department of Natural Resources. "Deer Hunting." Accessed March 18, 2025. https://www.dnr.state.mn.us/hunting/deer/index.html.

Morrill, Bruce. *Divine Worship and Human Healing: Liturgical Theology at the Margins of Life and Death*. Liturgical Press, 2009.

Morrill, Bruce. *Practical Sacramental Theology: At the Intersection of Liturgy and Ethics*. Cascade, 2021.

Morton, Lois Wright, and Troy C. Blanchard. "Starved for Access: Life in Rural America's Food Deserts." *Rural Realities* 1, no. 4 (2007): 1–10.

Most, Becca. "CSB/SJU Community Demands Action After Allegations of 'Sex Competition' Among Saint John's Students." *Saint Cloud Times*, October 21, 2021. https://www.sctimes.com/story/news/2021/10/21/students-demand-action-after-alleged-sex-competition-among-sju-students/8527264002/.

Mudd, Joseph C. *Eucharist as Meaning: Critical Metaphysics and Contemporary Sacramental Theology*. Liturgical Press, 2014.

Nakashima Brock, Rita. "The Pandemic Paradox: George Floyd, Moral Injury, and the Sustainability of Social Movements." In *Doing Theology in Pandemics: Facing Viruses, Violence, and Vitriol*, edited by Zachary Moon. Pickwick, 2022.

Newman, Ilana. "'Brain Gain' in Rural America and Who Is Behind It." *Daily Yonder*, March 13, 2024. https://dailyyonder.com/brain-gain-in-rural-america-and-who-is-behind-it/2024/03/13/.

North Dakota State Climate Office. "North Dakota Monthly Climate Summary." 17, no. 12 (December 2023). https://www.ndsu.edu/fileadmin/ndsco/ndsco/December23climate_final.pdf.

Orr, James. "JD Vance States the Obvious About *Ordo Amoris*." *First Things*, January 31, 2025. https://firstthings.com/jd-vance-states-the-obvious-about-ordo-amoris/.

Pinn, Anthony. *The End of God-Talk: An African-American Humanist Theology*. Oxford University, 2012.

Pope Francis. "For a Culture of Encounter." *L'Osservatore Romano*, weekly edition in English 38, September 23, 2016. https://www.vatican.va/content/francesco/en/cotidie/2016/documents/papa-francesco-cotidie_20160913_for-a-culture-of-encounter.html.

Pope, Stephen J. "The Problem with JD Vance's Theology of 'Ordo Amoris'—And Its Impact on Policy." *America*, February 13, 2025. https://www.americamagazine.org/faith/2025/02/13/ordo-amoris-stephen-pope-vance-249926.

Porter Stanley E., and Andrew W. Pitts. "Critical Realism in Context." *Journal for the Study of the Historical Jesus* 13 (2015): 276–306.

Prang, Allison. "JD Vance "Surprised" by Pushback from Pope, US Bishops on Immigration." *National Catholic Reporter*, February 28, 2025. https://www.ncronline.org/news/vance-surprised-pushback-pope-us-bishops-new-immigration-policies.

Pruitt, Lisa. "Mending the Rural-Urban Rift." Presentation. Westminster Town Hall Forum, Minneapolis, Minnesota, October 25, 2022. https://westminsterforum.org/forum/mending-the-rural-urban-rift/?fbclid=IwAR1kvnc9JPA4jjgGYC-8RXY-XWUHtSIyZC5hko0EMxNA3xvj9snx0zKf7QA.

Public Religion Research Institute and American Communities Project Staff. "Religious Stereotypes vs. Reality in Urban, Suburban, and Rural America." *American Communities Project*, April 15, 2022. https://www.americancommunities.org/religious-stereotypes-vs-reality-in-urban-suburban-and-rural-america/#:~:text=Rural%20and%20Working%20Class%20Country,and%2083%25%20of%20Evangelical%20Hubs.

Putnam, Robert D. *Bowling Alone: The Collapse and Revival of American Community*. Simon and Schuster, 2000.

Rahner, Karl. "The Theology of the Symbol." In *Theological Investigations*, vol. 5. Translated by Karl-H Kruger. Seabury, 1974.

Reimer-Barry, Emily. "Another Pro-Life Movement Is Possible." *CTSA Proceedings* 74 (2019): 21–41.

Rowlands, D. W., and Hannah Love. "Mapping Rural America's Diversity and Demographic Change." *Brookings*, September 28, 2021. https://www.brookings.edu/articles/mapping-rural-americas-diversity-and-demographic-change/.

Saliers, Don. *Worship as Theology: Foretaste of Glory Divine*. Abingdon, 1994.

Schadle, Matthew A. "Culture." In *Moral Agency Within Social Structures and Culture: A Primer on Critical Realism for Christian Ethics*, edited by Daniel K. Finn. Georgetown University, 2020.

Schaller, Thomas F., and Tom Waldman, *White Rural Rage: The Threat to American Democracy*. Random House, 2024.

Schmidt, Katherine G. *Virtual Communion: Theology of the Internet and the Catholic Sacramental Imagination*. Lexington/Fortress, 2020.

Schnell, Jan. "What Constitutes the Gathered Eucharistic Assembly?" *Currents in Theology and Mission* 50, no. 1 (2023): 42–47.

Schrag, Calvin O. *God as Otherwise than Being: Towards a Semantics of the Gift*. Northwestern University, 2002.

Seasoltz, R. Kevin. *God's Gift Giving: In Christ and Through the Spirit*. Continuum, 2007.

Sherr, Ian. "Tesla Drivers Are Getting Fed Up with Elon Musk's Twitter Meltdowns." CNET, December 23, 2022. https://www.cnet.com/tech/tesla-drivers-are-getting-fed-up-with-elon-musks-twitter-meltdowns/.

Sigmon, Casey T. "Failure to Discern the Online/Hybrid Body: A Captivity of the Eucharist." *Currents in Theology and Mission* 50, no. 1 (2023): 13–18.

Sinclair, Ward. "Melcher to Fight 'Zero-92' in Senate." *Washington Post*, September 20, 1987. https://www.washingtonpost.com/archive/politics/1987/09/20/melcher-to-fight-zero-92-in-senate/29a06ad5-7fb1-4449-b3fe-53caba755a81/.

Smith, Christian. *What Is a Person?: Rethinking Humanity, Social Life, and the Moral Good from the Person Up*. University of Chicago, 2010.

Stahl, William A. "Symbols and Ethics: An Approach to the Civil Religion Debate." *Union Seminary Quarterly Review* 34, no. 4 (1979): 229–238.

Stanton, Allen T. *Reclaiming Rural: Building Thriving Rural Congregations*. Rowman and Littlefield, 2021.

Stanton-Henry, Andy. *Recovering Abundance: Twelve Practices for Small-Town Leaders*. Fortress, 2022.

Steil, Mark. "Meat-Packing Plant Loses Workers to Immigration Raid." NPR, December 13, 2006. https://www.npr.org/2006/12/13/6620724/meat-packing-plant-loses-workers-to-immigration-raid.

"Support for Christian Nationalism in All 50 States: Findings from PRRI's 2023 American Values Atlas." *PRRI*, February 28, 2024. https://www.prri.org/research/support-for-christian-nationalism-in-all-50-states/.

Tan, Matthew John Paul. "Sarah Coakley and the Prayers of the Digital Body of Christ." In *Sarah Coakley and the Future of Systematic Theology*, edited by Janice McRandal. Fortress Press, 2016.

Turnbloom, David. "Liturgy in the Shadow of Trauma." *Religions* 13, no. 7 (2022): 583. https://doi.org/10.3390/rel13070583.

US Census Bureau. "Urban and Rural." Accessed March 18, 2025. https://www.census.gov/programs-surveys/geography/guidance/geo-areas/urban-rural.html.

US Department of Agriculture. "E-Connectivity for All Rural Americans Is a Modern-Day Necessity." Accessed March 18, 2025. https://www.usda.gov/broadband.

US Department of Agriculture Economic Research Service. "Rural Classifications: Overview." Accessed March 18, 2025. https://www.ers.usda.gov/topics/rural-economy-population/rural-classifications/.

US Department of Agriculture Economic Research Service. "What Is Rural?" Accessed March 18, 2025. https://www.ers.usda.gov/topics/rural-economy-population/rural-classifications/what-is-rural/.

US Department of Health and Human Services, National Institutes of Health. "Cyberbullying Linked with Suicidal Thoughts and Attempts in Young Adolescents." July 12, 2022. https://www.nih.gov/news-events/nih-research-matters/cyberbullying-linked-suicidal-thoughts-attempts-young-adolescents.

US Department of Justice, Office of Justice Programs, Bureau of Justice Statistics. *Criminal Victimization, 2022*. September 2023. https://bjs.ojp.gov/document/cv22.pdf.

US Health Resources and Services Administration. "Defining Rural Population." Accessed March 18, 2025. https://www.hrsa.gov/rural-health/about-us/what-is-rural.

Vaux, Kenneth. "Law and Lamb: AKEDAH and the Search for a Deep Religious Symbol for an Ecumenical Bioethics." *Christian Bioethics* 5, no. 3 (1999): 213–219.

West, Traci C. *Disruptive Christian Ethics: When Racism and Women's Lives Matter*. Westminster John Knox, 2006.

Westby, Joe. "The Rana Plaza Disaster: The Unholy Alliance of Business and Government in Bangladesh, and Around the World." Amnesty International, April 24, 2014. https://www.amnesty.org/en/latest/campaigns/2014/04/rana-plaza-disaster-the-unholy-alliance-of-business-and-government-in-bangladesh-and-around-the-world/.

Willman, Chris. "Jason Aldean's 'Try That in a Small Town' Video Undergoes Edits, Loses Footage of BLM Protests Used Without Permission." *Variety*, July 26, 2023. https://variety.com/2023/music/news/jason-aldean-video-edited-blm-footage-try-that-small-town-1235680869/.

Winchester, Ben. "A Rural Brain Gain Migration." University of Minnesota Extension. Accessed March 18, 2025. https://extension.umn.edu/economic-development/rural-brain-gain-migration.

Wirzba, Norman. *Agrarian Spirit: Cultivating Faith, Community, and the Land*. University of Notre Dame, 2022.

Wuthnow, Robert. *In the Blood: Understanding America's Farm Families*. Princeton University, 2015.

Wuthnow, Robert. *Small-Town America: Finding Community, Shaping the Future*. Princeton University, 2013.

Wuthnow, Robert. *Red State Religion: Faith and Politics in America's Heartland*. Princeton University, 2012.

Wuthnow, Robert. *Religion's Power: What Makes It Work*. Oxford University, 2023.

Wuthnow, Robert. *The Left Behind: Decline and Rage in Small-Town America*. Princeton University, 2018.

Yackel-Juleen, Mark L. *Everyone Must Eat: Food, Sustainability, and Ministry*. Fortress, 2021.

Zagzebski, Linda Trinkaus. *Epistemic Authority: A Theory of Trust, Authority, and Autonomy in Belief*. Oxford University, 2015.

INDEX